Distributional Consequences of Direct Foreign Investment

This is a volume in
ECONOMIC THEORY, ECONOMETRICS,
AND MATHEMATICAL ECONOMICS

A Series of Monographs and Textbooks

Consulting Editor: KARL SHELL

A complete list of titles in this series appears at the end of this volume.

Distributional Consequences of Direct Foreign Investment

ROBERT H. FRANK
DEPARTMENT OF ECONOMICS
CORNELL UNIVERSITY
ITHACA, NEW YORK

RICHARD T. FREEMAN
DIVISION OF INTERNATIONAL FINANCE
BOARD OF GOVERNORS OF THE FEDERAL RESERVE SYSTEM
WASHINGTON, D.C.

1978

ACADEMIC PRESS   New York   San Francisco   London
A Subsidiary of Harcourt Brace Jovanovich, Publishers

ACADEMIC PRESS, INC.
111 Fifth Avenue, New York, New York 10003

United Kingdom Edition published by
ACADEMIC PRESS, INC. (LONDON) LTD.
24/28 Oval Road, London NW1 7DX

Library of Congress Cataloging in Publication Data

Frank, Robert H
   The distributional consequences of direct
foreign investment.

   (Economic theory, econometrics, and mathematical economics series)
   Bibliography: p.
   1.   Investments, American––Mathematical models.
2.   Investments, Foreign and employment––United
States––Mathematical models.   I.   Freeman, Richard T.,
joint author.   II.   Title.
HG4538.F67   330.9'73'092   78–207
ISBN   0–12–265050–6

Contents

v

Preface

Rapid expansion of U.S. overseas investment through multinational corporations has been one of the most significant economic and political developments of the past twenty years. During that time one of the most controversial aspects of multinational operations has been the effect of overseas investment on the U.S. labor market. Allegations of runaway firms, estimates of extensive job loss, and attempts to restrict or further control the overseas activities of U.S. firms have been a regular feature of the debate over U.S. international economic policy in the 1960s and 1970s. In light of the higher levels of unemployment experienced in recent years, there is no reason to expect that the controversy will wane. Despite the intensity of the debate— or perhaps because of it—no clear resolution of the basic economic issues in this area has yet emerged.

Clearly, decisions on whether or not foreign investment merits more extensive control must turn on political judgments, as well as strictly economic considerations. Our focus in this study is on economic issues alone; we seek only to evaluate, to the extent that data permit, the merits of several of the fundamental economic questions that have been raised in this debate. A basic theme is that much of the current disagreement over such matters as the size of the job loss from foreign investment stems from the use of incorrect or inappropriate methods of analysis. Accordingly, we have tried to demonstrate here how this and related issues can be analyzed by building from basic economic principles. Inadequate data—access to much of which is controlled by the multinationals themselves—have hindered most previous research in this area. In this regard our study, with its very tentative quantitative findings, is subject to similar limitations. With these constraints in mind we stress that the results of this study are primarily illustrative. However, the methods developed here, we feel, can be usefully applied as the data base continues to expand.

A number of colleagues have been kind enough to review and offer comments on parts of this study as the work progressed. Special thanks are due to Ned Gramlich, Harry Grubert, Arnold Harberger, Tom Horst, Charles Kindleberger, Robert Lipsey, Peggy Musgrave, Anthony Scaperlanda, Guy Stevens, and various members of the Federal Reserve and Cornell University staffs who have alerted us to a number of pitfalls. We grant them, of course, the customary exemption from responsibility for any errors that may remain. We also wish to express our thanks to Chris Delgado, Amihai Glazer, Joel Greer, Robert Kalish, Mateen Thobani, Jaime Willars, and Shirley Graham for their invaluable assistance in researching and preparing earlier manuscripts.

Parts of this study were supported by grants from the U.S. Departments of Labor, State, and Treasury. The views expressed here, however, are the authors' own and should be taken neither as those of the sponsoring institutions nor of the institutions with which we are currently affiliated.

Distributional Consequences of Direct Foreign Investment

Chapter I

Introduction

In the current discussion of the tax treatment of multinational firms' overseas activities, a central issue has been the question of what effect these activities have on domestic employment and income. Management's claim that overseas activities help create U.S. jobs is greeted by labor's counterclaim that such activities result in the wholesale export of U.S. jobs.[1] Although the public debate on this question has been intense, highly partisan arguments have tended to obscure the underlying economic issues. In this study we have developed an analytical framework that clarifies these issues and that can be used to evaluate the net effect of overseas investment on both U.S. employment demand in the short run and on the level and distribution of domestic income in

[1] Numerical estimates of the effect of direct foreign investment range from the U.S. Tariff Commission finding that American investment abroad may have wiped out as many as 1.3 million U.S. jobs (U.S. Tariff Commission, 1973) to the calculation of a Harvard Business School study that the same investments were responsible for the creation of 600,000 jobs (Stobaugh *et al.*, 1972).

the long run. To illustrate how this methodology can be applied, we also provide some sample estimates for recent years using the limited data that are currently available.

From a conceptual point of view, short-run job loss estimates are net figures in the sense that they represent differences between positive and negative contributions of multinational corporations (MNCs) to domestic production employment. The principal negative contribution can be expressed as the fraction of foreign subsidiary employment that could have been retained in the United States had the MNC attempted to serve foreign markets by exporting from domestic production sites. In our study we term this the "export displacement" effect.

Other authors have mentioned several possible sources of positive effects of direct foreign investment (DFI) on domestic employment that work to offset this export displacement. Foremost among these is the effect of subsidiary demands for U.S. exports of intermediate products,[2] which we designate as the "export stimulus" effect. In this study we shall focus on these two main production related effects.

In general, subsidiary imports from U.S. parents and other U.S. firms account for only a small fraction of subsidiary net sales (4 % for all industries in 1970).[3] Accordingly, the conventional procedure of calculating the export stimulus effect as the employment required to produce these exports has generated relatively little controversy.

Calculation of the export displacement effect, however, is an altogether different matter. A very simple version of the export displacement effect may be written as

$$\Delta L = \sigma \times \Delta Q_F \times l, \tag{1}$$

[2] Other employment stimulating effects which have been noted include increased (white-collar) employment in domestic MNC headquarters, increased employment associated with export of complementary MNC products, and additional domestic employment stimulated indirectly by increased incomes and export demand abroad—all of which are likely to be of second-order significance when compared to the direct, production-related effects on which we focus in this study. For more detail on these and related issues, see U.S. Tariff Commission, (1973), Hawkins (1972b), and Horst (1974).

[3] Based on firms sampled in the Department of Commerce *Special Survey of U.S. Multinational Companies for 1970.*

where

ΔL is the number of jobs lost,

ΔQ_F is the increase in subsidiary output that results from a direct foreign investment,

l is the labor–output ratio in the firm's production process, and

σ is the fraction of subsidiary sales that could have been served by exporting from the domestic production site.

Written in this fashion, the export displacement effect ranges from a low of zero to a high value equal to the total increase in subsidiary employment as the substitution parameter, sigma, ranges in value between 0 and 1. The controversy about whether DFI stimulates or retards domestic employment thus turns on differences in judgment about the value of this key substitution parameter.[4]

For this reason, our study begins in Chapter II with a survey of existing studies of the DFI phenomenon that critically evaluates any evidence that bears on the question of what firms would or could have done in the absence of a direct foreign investment alternative. Much has been written on this issue and a variety of analytical approaches has been employed in its study. We examine closely several survey investigations, individual firm case studies, and formal econometric models and conclude that existing studies provide very little useful information on the crucial question of what would have happened in the absence of a direct investment option.

In Chapter III we develop an alternative framework within which to estimate the degree of substitutability of home for foreign production. This framework consists of a microeconomic model of the multinational firm as it operates under two alternative policy regimes. The first regime places no restrictions on the firm's activities while the

---

[4] Precisely this point was made in a recent study by Musgrave, which asserted that "The effects of direct foreign investment made abroad on the U.S. economy will very largely depend on whether or not such investment is apt to be a substitute for investment in the home economy. It was also noted that to the best of the author's knowledge little if any empirical research has been directed to this specific question." (Musgrave, 1975, p. 124.)

second denies it the option of establishing a foreign production subsidiary. The home–foreign production substitution parameter is taken as the ratio of the firm's domestic production level under the constrained regime to its foreign production level in the unconstrained regime. Viewed in this fashion, the substitution parameter is seen to depend on foreign and domestic cost conditions, foreign market demand conditions, taxes, and transport and tariff costs. For the most empirically relevant case of constant marginal costs in manufacturing industries, we show that the calculation of the substitution parameter requires only that the ratio of marginal costs in the two production sites, foreign market demand elasticity, and tariff and transport costs be known. Procedures for using existing data sources to generate these magnitudes are described. Sample estimates of the substitution parameters are presented for the major manufacturing industries in our study.

In Chapter IV we show how the highly simplified model of Chapter III can be extended to deal with more complex cases.

In Chapter V we use input–output techniques, together with information on substitutability from Chapter III, to obtain estimates of the net employment impact of direct foreign investment. One of the useful features of this approach is that it allows us to consider separately both the export displacement and export stimulus contributions to employment in each industry, taking into account both primary and secondary effects through the I–O matrix. Since the reliability of our estimates is uncertain, we also calculate values for a "break-even" sigma—i.e., the sigma value for which the net employment effect is exactly zero. By comparing our estimated values for sigma with this break-even value, it appears that the net employment impact of DFI is likely to be a substantial short-run job loss.

In Chapter VI we present estimates in which the employment-demand effects of DFI are broken down by occupational category. We employ these estimates to examine the question of what effect foreign investments have on the problem of structural bottlenecks in the composition of the domestic demand for labor. We conclude that DFI exacerbates such bottlenecks slightly by causing much larger reductions in blue collar than in white collar employment demands.

Our calculations of the net job displacement effects present only part of the picture of the impact of DFI on unemployment in the industries and occupations considered in our study. Policymakers concerned with the effects of overseas investments on domestic labor markets must consider not only the extent of the initial dislocations, i.e., our net job displacement figures, but also the speed with which these dislocations tend to equilibrate over time. Displacements which occur in an industry in which job seekers are quickly relocated will generate less policy concern, for example, than those occurring in industries in which job seekers secure placement only with great difficulty and delay.

We approach this issue in Chapter VII within the framework of a probabilistic model of an industry labor market. For each of eight large manufacturing industries we use this model to simulate the labor market adjustment dynamics that occur in response to hypothetical job displacements equal in magnitude to those that we calculate in Chapter V using the 1970 DFI vector. One of the most striking outcomes of this simulation exercise is that, in each of the industries we examine, most workers who are displaced as a result of DFI are observed to have found new jobs within eight weeks of the onset of their unemployment. We conclude from this pattern that, at least when aggregate demand is at 1970 levels, widespread incidence of protracted unemployment spells is not one of the most important adjustment costs of DFI-related job displacements.

Our analysis through Chapter VII is primarily microeconomic in character. While this focus is appropriate for shorter-run issues, it is clearly less so when the time horizon is extended. Given time, the aggregate economy can adjust to job losses caused by DFI through either market forces or direct policy intervention. Accordingly, analysis of the long-term implications of DFI should focus on its effects on equilibrium wages, income shares, and output, rather than temporary job losses. In Chapter VIII we present a highly aggregated model that can be used to analyze the main features of an ongoing foreign investment program and its effect on the domestic economy. We conclude that, when account is taken of the leakage of tax revenues into the treasuries of host countries, foreign investment results in a slightly lower level of equilibrium U.S. national income. As far as the distribution of income is concerned, the principal long-run consequence of DFI appears to be a moderate shift favoring capital. These findings depend, however, on the assumption of a constant aggregate savings propensity. When the propensity to save is affected by foreign investment, the outcome is less clear.

Licensing agreements are a principal alternative mechanism to DFI whereby U.S. technologies are transferred abroad. In Chapter VIII we also employ a modified version of the aggregate model to examine the effect of technology transfer through licensing on the size and composition of domestic income. Unlike DFI, licensing does not involve the export of U.S. capital to a foreign subsidiary. Accordingly, tax payments to host country governments are much smaller under licensing than under direct investment. As a result, we find that technology transfer yields a small increase in domestic income. As in the case of DFI, we find that technology transfer through licensing results in a slight shift toward capital in the distribution of domestic income.

In Chapter IX we highlight the principal findings of our study and note briefly some of its policy implications.

Chapter II

Literature Survey

The literature that deals with the effects of DFI on the level of employment demand in the United States is large and highly diverse, as much so in its methods of analysis as in its conclusions. Before exploring in detail specific studies that deal directly with the question of the substitutability of home for foreign investment, we present a very brief background discussion that conveys a broad outline of the nature of the phenomenon with which we are dealing.

Students of the multinational corporation are well aware that these organizations tend to be extremely large in size. A 1970 Department of Commerce survey revealed that 298 U.S. firms with 5237 foreign affiliates accounted for 55 % of total foreign affiliate assets and employed an estimated 62 % of all persons employed in U.S. foreign affiliates, some 3 million persons.

Though many discussions of the DFI phenomenon tend to emphasize cases in which firms have fled to low wage areas in order to escape high labor costs in the United States, the largest share of American investments abroad is in fact concentrated in Europe and Canada, where unit labor costs do not differ substantially from those in the United States.[1]

The output of foreign affiliates is, with some exceptions—most notably in the electronic components industry and Canadian subsidiaries in general—sold almost entirely in foreign markets. Foreign affiliates outside of Canada exported only about 2% of their sales to the United States during the 1960s. In 1970 all imports from subsidiaries amounted to only 0.7% of total U.S. production.[2]

Though there are many obvious and important exceptions that should be borne in mind, there does appear to be sufficient evidence to warrant characterizing a typical multinational firm as a large, technology-intensive organization whose foreign affiliates produce and sell differentiated products in the large markets of highly industrialized economies.[3] This characterization of the multinational firm underlies much of our thinking as we turn now to the evaluation of specific studies.

Survey Studies

Typical of the survey research method is a 1972 study by the Business International Corporation.[4] B.I.C. approached highly placed executives with 35 firms having foreign affiliates and asked: "Do you believe your U.S. exports would have been higher, lower, or about the same in 1970 had you not invested abroad in the 1960s?" Of the 33 executives who responded, 30 answered that exports would have been lower, two estimated no change in exports, while only one had the opinion that his firm's exports would have been higher had they not invested abroad. Polk, Meister, and Veit, in their 1966 study,[5] examine survey data supplied by National Industrial Conference Board firms and find that these respondents also stress the defensive nature of overseas

---

[1] See, e.g., U.S. Tariff Commission (1973 pp. 97, 634).

[2] See Emergency Committee on American Trade (1973).

[3] See Hymer and Rowthorne (1970) and Vernon (1973).

[4] *The Effects of U.S. Corporate Foreign Investment, 1960–1970* (Business International Corporation, 1972).

[5] *U.S. Production Abroad and the Balance of Payments* (Polk et al., 1966).

investments. Other survey studies, such as the National Foreign Trade Council's,[6] report much the same findings, but it is our judugment that information of this type is of very limited usefulness as evidence on the question of what would have happened in the absence of direct foreign investment alternatives. Executives of MNC's have long been aware of critics' claims that foreign activities impact adversely on domestic employment and the balance of payments and that, in recent years, organized labor and others have been lobbying in support of such measures as the Burke–Hartke Bill, which would impose specific restrictions on direct foreign investment activities. Except for the fact that many of the survey studies were commissioned and supported by management organizations, one would be at a loss to explain how so many researchers could be oblivious to the palpable self-interest of MNC executives in portraying their foreign activities in as favorable a light as possible vis-a-vis their impact on the domestic economy.

An equal measure of skepticism must be brought to a reading of research findings gathered by organized labor on the question of how DFI affects the level of domestic employment. "Evidence" in the AFL-CIO's "A Program to Build America's Jobs and Trade in the Seventies" consists largely of a series of cases in which jobs were said to have been exported from the United States.

> 600 machinists' jobs in Elmira, N.Y. were exported from the United States when the Remington Rand typewriter plant, which once employed over 6000, closed in 1972. High costs and imports were some of the many factors cited by the local manager for the shutdown. Some production was moved to Canada. But this year the local union reported that some of the machinery was sent to Brazil, where Sperry Rand, the multinational owner of Remington Rand, also has an interest. Typewriters made under license to Remington Rand specifications in Japan have been imported. The Elmira machinists joined an estimated 30,000 other typewriter employees in Missouri, Connecticut and other states whose jobs were exported in the five years before 1972. (AFL-CIO, 1973, p. 39)

---

[6] *Impact of U.S. Direct Foreign Investment on U.S. Employment and Trade* (National Foreign Trade Council, 1971).

Such examples ignore completely the question of what alternatives existed for Remington. Did cost conditions in the Elmira Plant permit the manufacture of typewriters at a price competitive with imported typewriters? Or did relocating production abroad simply facilitate Remington's continued participation in a market it would otherwise have lost to foreigners? If the AFL-CIO case histories are meant only to illustrate that DFI activities are often accompanied by job displacements that point up a need for compensatory labor market policies, they are successful; but they are simply not responsive to the question of how many of the lost jobs would have survived under a regime in which DFI were prohibited.

Statistical Tabulations

Several studies have employed elementary statistical procedures in an attempt to cast light on the relationship between DFI and domestic employment. A National Association of Manufacturers research paper makes the point that those firms with the greatest level of DFI activity are the same firms which have experienced the most extensive growth in domestic employment levels. In their recent *Survey of Current Business* article, Kraseman and Barker have produced considerable documentation for this claim (see Table 1). Employing the D.O.C. survey of 298 U.S. MNCs cited earlier, they calculate that domestic employment for all industries grew from 1966 to 1970 at a rate of 2.7% compared with 1.8% for all U.S. firms (noting that some, but not all, of the greater domestic employment growth is accounted for by greater MNC merger and acquisition activities). Moreover, they point out, this employment growth rate differential is observed for nearly every industry examined in their sample. Hawkins (1972a), further documents the high positive correlation between domestic and foreign economic activity levels.

One extreme example of the type of inference researchers have drawn from these statistical studies may be seen in the following statement in the Business International Corporation report cited earlier:

If there is any validity to the job export hypothesis, then the firms in the sample in this study should have been exporting jobs with

TABLE 1

Employment of all U.S. firms and of MNCs in sample, by industry

	All U.S. firms			U.S. reporters in 1970 sample survey			All areas		
	1966	1970	Average annual rate of growth, 1966–1970(%)	1966	1970	Average annual rate of growth, 1966–1970(%)	1966	1970	Average annual rate of growth, 1966–1970(%)
	(thousands)			(thousands)			(thousands)		
All private industry	57,259	61,486	1.8	7968	8851	2.7	2412	2970	5.3
Manufacturing	19,095	19,224	0.2	5885	6335	1.9	1704	2156	6.1
Food products	1779	1784	0.1	235	260	2.6	119	141	4.3
Chemicals and allied products	966	1054	2.2	665	725	2.2	220	250	3.2
Primary and fabricated metals	2702	2698	0	709	724	0.5	86	103	4.6
Machinery	3831	3906	0.5	1617	1860	3.6	555	731	7.1
Transportation equipment	2210	2063	-1.7	1681	1568	-1.7	421	546	6.7
Other	7607	7719	0.4	978	1198	5.2	303	385	6.2
Petroleum	486	480	-0.2	479	522	2.2	296	271	-2.2
Other industries	37,678	41,782	2.6	1604	1994	5.6	411	542	7.2
Mining	349	357	0.6	a	91	a	79	74	-1.6
Trade	13,329	15,108	3.2	516	589	3.4	169	308	16.2
Other	24,000	26,317	2.3	a	1314	a	163	161	a

SOURCE: Kraseman and Barker (1973). Data from U.S. Department of Commerce, Bureau of Economic Analysis, International Investment Division and National Income and Wealth Division.

a Suppressed to avoid disclosure of data for individual reporters.

11

great abandon during past years. The number of employees of these companies must have fallen quite drastically during the 1960–1970 period. Certainly the firms in the sample should show a much slower rate of increase in the U.S. than all manufacturers in the U.S.

None of these assumptions is true. Indeed, the sample increased employment in the U.S. during 1960–1970 far faster than did U.S. manufacturing industry as a whole. ... These comparisons again indicate that the job export hypothesis is without factual foundation.[7]

Such remarks betray a misunderstanding of the relationship between statistical correlation and causality. That the level of DFI activity and growth in domestic employment are positively associated across firms and industries is in no way indicative that high employment growth rates are the *result* of high levels of DFI. One might be inclined to view such a correlation as suggestive of a causal relationship if all firms were alike in every respect save for the level at which they pursue DFI activities (though we shall argue later that for firms to be alike in all respects other than DFI should result in their having equal DFI flows as well), but this is most clearly not the case. As the AFL-CIO points out, firms that invest heavily abroad include "America's largest concerns, which are the largest employers, the largest defense contractors, i.e., these firms are not a cross section. They are the commanding heights of our industrial structure" (AFL-CIO, 1973, p. 19). The same features, in other words, which place firms in concentrated, high-growth, high-technology industries may at the same time be features that lead naturally to participation in international investment ventures. Statistical investigations of the DFI-domestic employment relationship that fail to control for important characteristics that differentiate firms tell us very little about what would have happened had firms been denied a DFI option.

Several studies have approached the question of what effect DFI has on the domestic labor market by considering a range of assumptions as to the nature of the domestic production alternatives that exist for firms that invest abroad. The most comprehensive of these studies is a 1973 report sponsored by the U.S. Tariff Commission.

---

[7] Reprinted from *The Effects of U.S. Corporate Foreign Investment, 1960–1970*, p. 8, with permission of the publisher, Business International Corporation, New York.

The Tariff Commission report considers first a set of assumptions favorable to the position of MNC critics, namely, that in the absence of the foreign production facility no similar facility would have been built by foreign competitors, and that the markets now served by MNC foreign affiliates could have been served at identical prices by U.S.-produced goods. Under these premises, data are employed from the Commerce Department's 1966 Benchmark Survey of MNCs and the 1970 sample followup to that survey to calculate that a "gross job-loss" figure of 2.4 million jobs is attributable to the cumulative total of all DFI that had taken place through 1970. From this gross job-loss figure a series of offsets was deducted representing

(1)   U.S. employment required to manage and service overseas affiliates;

(2)   U.S. employment involved in manufacturing goods exported to the MNCs overseas affiliates;

(3)   U.S. employment required to manufacture goods which satisfy the additional foreign demand for U.S. exports that stems from the contribution of MNCs to the growth of foreign income; and

(4)   the U.S. employment of foreign-based MNCs.

The offsets total 1.1 million jobs, leaving a "net job impact" of 1.3 million jobs, which the report offers as an upper limit for the extent of job loss associated with the foreign operations of U.S.-based MNCs.

Next the report relaxes the assumption that 100 % of the subsidiaries' sales could be served from U.S. production, and assumes instead that only half of the foreign markets could be so served; this adjustment results in a reduction of the net job loss figure to just over 400,000 jobs. A final set of estimates is calculated based on the assumption that, in the absence of a foreign production option, U.S. exporters could have maintained the share of world trade in manufacturing that they held during 1960–1961, a benchmark period chosen because it precedes much of the most recent upsurge in DFI activity. From the number of jobs associated with these particular export assumptions, the report then deducts the estimates of U.S. employment accounted for by the overseas activities by U.S. MNCs (the "offsets," calculated as in the preceding cases). This exercise produces the conclusion that the cumulative impact of DFI through 1970 was the production of a net job *gain* of 500,000 jobs in the United States. The preparers of the Tariff

Commision Report express a mild preference for the latter set of figures as representing the most realistic of the three.

In an earlier study Hawkins (1972b) uses procedures quite similar to those employed in the Tariff Commission report in examining aggregate data for the manufacturing sector. Like the researchers who carried out the Tariff Commission study, Hawkins discovers that the sign and size of the net job displacement effect of DFI is very sensitive to assumptions about what the alternatives to overseas production really are for U.S. MNCs—his results range from a net creation of 240,000 jobs to a net loss of 660,000 jobs. Hawkins' judgment is that "the probable net employment effect was approximately a 'wash'— i.e., displacement was equaled by jobs created within a range of 25,000 jobs" (Hawkins, 1972b, p. 8).

It is difficult to fault both the Hawkins study and the Tariff Commission Report for adopting the modest goal of attempting to present the range of possible net job displacement outcomes which correspond to various assumptions about the degree of substitutability of home for foreign production. The studies have quite successfully shown that there is ample room for debate concerning the effects of DFI on domestic labor demands. Indeed, as we shall argue in Chapter V, by failing to consider the effects of domestic interindustry flows associated with DFI-induced production changes, the Hawkins and Tariff Commission studies have actually *understated* the range of possible outcomes by a very substantial margin.

The Product-Cycle Literature

The product-cycle literature[8] presents a qualitative rationale and description of the direct foreign investment process that many have found plausible. This literature begins by noting that, to a very large degree, MNCs produce and sell in markets which can be characterized as oligopolistic; goods typically are technology intensive and display a substantial measure of product differentiation; scale economies are fully exploited only at production levels that correspond to sizeable shares of total industry output. When such firms first attempt to introduce their products into new markets overseas, scale economy con-

---

[8] See, for example, Vernon (1966) and Gruber *et al.* (1967).

siderations, not to mention the issue of risk, firmly dictate the United States as the optimal production location. As the overseas market expands and becomes more secure, however, scale economies become possible in foreign sites and the firm is then faced with a choice of where to locate production facilities. While avoidance of transport costs, tariff barriers, and other factors may point to a preference for the foreign site, the firm still has the option, which for a variety of reasons it may elect to exercise, of continuing to serve the foreign market by exporting from the U.S. production site. As time passes, however, the range of options facing the MNC tends to narrow, according to this view. For a given product, the pace of technical innovation diminishes through time and, as this happens, barriers to foreign competition tend to weaken. Products produced abroad by foreign concerns tend to be regarded as increasingly close substitutes for the product of the U.S. firm, and, as foreign producers become more technologically proficient, tariff and transport costs become an unsustainable burden on products produced in the United States for export. Ultimately the U.S. firm must either concentrate production for the foreign market entirely in the foreign site and compete with foreign rivals for a share of that market in much the same way as it competes in the United States with U.S. rivals or be forced to withdraw from the foreign market entirely.

Accordingly, the effect on domestic employment demand of denying the firm a direct foreign investment option will be different in different stages of the product cycle. In the initial stage of the cycle, denial of the DFI option will, of course, have no impact since overseas production would not be observed during this stage in any event. During the intermediate stage, a restriction of foreign investment will stimulate domestic employment by forcing the firm to serve the foreign market by exporting from its U.S. production site. By contrast, however, a ban on foreign production sites imposed during the final stage of the product cycle would not serve to stimulate production in the United States; its effect would instead be simply to eliminate the U.S. firm from any form of participation in the foreign market.

While in general we feel the product-cycle literature offers a useful description of some of the important dynamic processes involved in the DFI phenomenon, it is best to keep in mind that even rather minor changes in assumptions and emphasis can lead to substantial variations in the ultimate outcome of the product cycle story. It is by no means clear, for example, that the pace of technical advance in a given product line exhibits a systematic tendency to diminish through time, resulting in a corresponding decay of product differentiation. Nor is it clear that other sources of product differentiation, most notably advertising and other marketing activities, could not be employed indefinitely to maintain a considerable degree of brand loyalty even with the emergence of an increasing array of foreign-produced substitutes. Given also the fact that trade barriers have eroded considerably through time, only those firms whose products are very expensive to transport or whose fabrication may be accomplished using productive factors markedly less expensive than those available in the United States are likely to face the limited set of long-run options described in the product-cycle literature. Surely there exist large numbers of firms for whom the option of serving foreign markets either from a domestic or overseas production site will continue to remain viable well into the future.

Case Evaluations

In a 1972 study, Robert Stobaugh and associates from the Harvard Business School examined specific direct foreign investment projects for nine different firms, one from each of nine two-digit industries that account for the bulk of U.S. overseas manufacturing affiliate activity. Descriptive summary information concerning the projects considered by the Stobaugh group appears in Table 2.

The Harvard Business School researchers approached the question of what effects DFI has on the domestic economy within a well-defined prior conceptual framework, which is essentially an extension of the product-cycle hypothesis described above.

The United States because of its large population and relatively high per capita income is the world's largest market for most new products. As firms generate new products in response to stimuli from markets, most new products are developed by firms in close contact with the U.S. market. The overwhelming majority of these are U.S.-owned. These manufacturers typically locate their initial plants in the United States in order to minimize communication costs within the firm, with customers, and with suppliers during

TABLE 2

Characteristics of foreign direct investments selected for nine case studies

Industry from which case selected (SIC No.)	Ownership	Existing or new subsidiary	Primary market planned to be served by investment	Size of project ($ million)	Geographic location of investment		
					Canada	Other developed countries	Less developed countries
Food products (20)	Joint venture	New	Third country	1			Africa
Paper and allied products (26)	Wholly owned	Existing	Local	20	Canada		
Chemicals and allied products (28)	Joint venture	New and expansion	Local	25		Japan	
Petroleum (29)	Wholly owned	New and expansion	Third country	195		Europe[a]	
Rubber products (30)	Wholly owned	Existing	Local	8	Canada		
Primary and fabricated metals (33, 34)	Wholly owned (later joint venture)	New	Local	5			Latin America
Nonelectrical machinery (35)	Wholly owned	New and expansion	Local and third country	55		Europe	
Electrical machinery (36)	Wholly owned	New	United States	5			S.E. Asia
Transportation equipment (37)	Wholly owned	New	Local	16			S.E. Asia

SOURCE: Stobaugh and Associates (1972, p. 5).
[a] Investment also includes oil tankers.

17

the time the product is nonstandardized and production techniques likely to change rapidly. As a result of this pattern, the U.S. has been the leader in new product development. The U.S. firms subsequently begin exporting these products. At this stage of the industry's development, the U.S. has 100 percent of the world's production and exports.

Later, production begins in other major industrial nations, sometimes by indigenous firms and sometimes by U.S. firms sensing a threat to their export market. As a result, the share of world production made in the United States begins to decline, and as foreign exports begin, the share of world exports made in the U.S. begins to decline. Regardless of whether U.S. firms or indigenous firms are the first to produce outside the U.S., indigenous firms eventually begin production as the technology becomes more widely diffused. Thus, the share of world production made by U.S. multinational enterprises declines.

Late in the product and industry life cycle competition becomes much keener and cost considerations more important. At this stage, production commences in countries with low costs for export to other countries. Usually the low-cost factor is labor, but in some cases it is raw materials.

If the U.S. firms failed to invest abroad, then they would retain less of the world market. (Stobaugh *et al.*, 1972, p. 6)

Armed with this view of the DFI process, the Stobaugh team interviewed company executives and examined company records, whereupon an assumption was made concerning what each firm's alternative to the DFI project was. The details of how these critical assumptions were arrived at are not provided in their report, but *in every case* the researchers concluded that in the absence of the DFI project *the foreign market would be lost entirely* to overseas competitors within at most a five year period and in most instances much more rapidly. Based on these assumptions about alternatives, the report then calculates the time profiles of project impacts on domestic employment and the balance of payments. In seven of the nine cases the net domestic employment effects are computed to be positive from the beginning; net employment effects are negative during the initial stages of the other two projects considered but the negative components of these effects decay to zero, leaving only a positive stream of employment effects of DFI as in the other seven cases.

Horst has criticized the Stobaugh study primarily on the grounds that the cases considered do not really appear to constitute a representative sample of the universe of firms with overseas affiliates.

> From what is known about the "universe" of foreign investments, this particular sample seems somewhat biased towards less-developed countries and low-technology products. Having recently completed a study of the food-processing industry, this author was more than a little surprised to find the case of a farm and cannery in Africa. Most outstanding food-processing investments are selling highly advertised convenience and snack foods to growing middle-class markets abroad, not extracting raw materials from remote countries. In the high-technology industries—chemicals, machinery, and electric equipment—the first case is drawn from the one country, Japan, having strongest restrictions on foreign investing, while the latter two both involve products at the low end of the product-cycle. Where in the Stobaugh study are the high-technology products in the developed countries, i.e., the cases where firms may really have a difficult choice between exporting and investing? The sample also seems biased towards the Far East and Africa (four out of nine cases), where less than 15% of outstanding investments in 1968 were located. (Horst, 1974, p. 37)

Neglecting the issue of the representativeness of the Stobaugh group's sample, we are inclined to remain quite skeptical about the conclusions drawn from the individual cases themselves. The unanimously positive employment effects reported in the Harvard Study, which, as we noted earlier, was conducted under an a priori conceptual framework which strongly favors positive employment effects, depend almost entirely on the case evaluators' *assumptions* about the nature of the firm's alternatives to foreign production sites. To be able to evaluate the results of the Stobaugh study at all, it is necessary that detailed information be made available concerning the data and methods employed by the researchers in formulating these assumptions about foreign production alternatives. The failure of the Stobaugh study to provide this information severely limits its usefulness as evidence concerning the substitutability of home for foreign investment.

Econometric Studies

The net effect of the direct foreign investment option on domestic employment is the sum of several conflicting effects and is impossible to predict from a priori considerations. Accordingly, it is not surprising that many researchers have approached the DFI-domestic activity relationship from an econometric point of view. Taken as a whole, recent studies of the DFI-domestic activity relationship represent attempts by researchers to improve upon the post hoc, ergo propter hoc reasoning of the tabular studies cited earlier. Trying to control for as many factors as possible, researchers have employed regression analysis to determine the degree of association between DFI and various measures of domestic economic activity (e.g., domestic investment and exports). After mentioning the results of some of these efforts below, we will argue that the econometric approach, as it might conceivably be implemented with currently available data, promises to shed very little light on the "what would have happened otherwise?" question.

One of the simplest studies, by Herring and Willett (1973), uses aggregate time series data for the manufacturing sector, and regresses DFI (defined as subsidiary plant and equipment expenditures) on domestic plant and equipment investment and a linear time trend. They find that an additional $1 million of domestic investment is associated with an additional $1.38 million in direct foreign investment.

In a much more detailed study Lipsey and Weiss (1972) have analyzed the relationship between exports and foreign investments using Department of Commerce data for individual firms. Partitioning their sample of U.S. subsidiaries by country, Lipsey and Weiss observe that the level of subsidiary activity in a given country exhibits no systematic association with the level of U.S. exports to that country (though subsidiary activity is, they note, negatively related to third-country exports to the subsidiary's host country).

Thomas Horst, in a study of United States–Canada trade and investment data (1972a), established that the share of the Canadian market for a product that is served by an American industry, either by export or by affiliate production in Canada, is more closely related to the industry's research and development activity than either the share of exports or the share of subsidiary sales. Horst interprets this result as "indirect evidence that exporting and subsidiary production represent alternative means of exploiting technology in the Canadian market."

Horst contradicts this finding in a more recent paper (1974), which embodies the most comprehensive effort which has been yet made to control for firm characteristics in regression studies of industry export measures and industry foreign subsidiary activity. Using industry-by-country data from the 1966 Department of Commerce Benchmark Census of U.S. MNCs, Horst begins with the preliminary exercise, interesting in its own right, of regressing deflated industry export rates on variables measuring the level of industry research and development expenditures, advertising expenditures, mean value of firm assets, foreign market size and characteristics, and dummies for the machinery and producer goods industries, in which American firms are presumed to have unusually great technological advantage. Horst observes that the coefficients on these variables in general have the expected signs and concludes that "the origins of American competitive advantage can be identified statistically. We are thus in a position to determine how American exports vary with subsidiary net sales, holding these common causes constant." Horst then proceeds to add a subsidiary sales regressor to his preliminary regression equation and finds that its coefficient is positive and statistically significant at conventional levels. Horst concludes that: "The complementarities between net sales by manufacturing affiliates abroad and exports of either the parent firm or all firms in the industry have tended to outweigh the substitutional effects."

If one is prepared to agree with Horst's results, his findings are extremely significant, for they imply at least the direction, if not the magnitude, of the net job displacement effect of DFI. The question of how the association between foreign subsidiary and domestic activity variables observed in regression analysis is properly interpreted as evidence on the "what would have happened otherwise?" issue is of crucial importance for our study and must be considered with great care.

In order to answer such a question, it is fruitful first to examine the underlying behavioral relationships that have generated the data on which the regression studies are based. We begin with a simple model of a firm trying to maximize profits subject to constraint, and focus on the choice of optimal export and foreign subsidiary production flows. In this framework the firm's goal is to maximize

$$\Pi = \Pi(Q_H, Q_F, Z) \tag{1}$$

with respect to Q_H, Q_F, and Z, where Π is total profits; Q_H domestic production for export, Q_F foreign subsidiary production, and Z other choice variables.

Subject to standard production and demand constraints, this optimization is presumed to yield unique solutions Q_H^*, Q_F^* and Z^*.

In the framework of this simple model, the question of what would have happened in the absence of a direct foreign investment alternative may be posed in the following form: If the level of foreign subsidiary production is constrained to be below its unconstrained optimal value, how is the optimal value of domestic production for export affected? If this constrained value of the foreign subsidiary production level is denoted as $\tilde{Q}_F$, we observe that the maximization exercise (1) above is reduced by one dimension and the optimal export flow now exhibits an explicit dependence on the value of the constrained foreign production level, $\tilde{Q}_F$. We represent this dependence as

$$\tilde{Q}_H^* = \tilde{Q}_H^*(\tilde{Q}_F). \tag{2}$$

For incremental changes in the value of the constrained foreign production level, the net substitutability of home for foreign production is[9]

$$\tilde{\sigma} = -\frac{\partial \tilde{Q}_H^*}{\partial \tilde{Q}_F}. \tag{3}$$

Alternatively, if the constraint completely prohibits foreign subsidiary production (i.e., if $\tilde{Q}_F = 0$), a modified version of (3) may be employed:

$$\tilde{\sigma} = \frac{\tilde{Q}_H^*(0) - Q_H^*}{Q_F^*}. \tag{3'}$$

If foreign and domestic production activities are net complements, expressions (3) and (3') will be negative; positive if they are substitutes.

---

[9] The expression $\tilde{\sigma}$ differs from the substitution parameter σ as defined in Chapter I; $\tilde{\sigma}$ represents the net result of all offsetting effects associated with subsidiary operations, whereas σ deals only with the size of the export displacement effect.

It is quickly observed from our simple model that an estimating equation for export flows would *not* properly include variable measuring foreign subsidiary production levels unless, for some reason, externally imposed constraints on these cause them to enter directly into the determination of Q_H^*. To our knowledge, there have been no effective, systematic constraints of this type on output levels of subsidiaries of U.S. MNCs.[10] In the absence of such constraints, both Q_F^* and Q_H^* are choice variables for the firm, as it seeks to maximize its objective function.

What is the result, then, of employing a foreign subsidiary production variable as a regressor in an estimating equation for export flows? For purposes of illustration, suppose we introduce the subsidiary production variable into the export equation as follows:

$$Q_H = X\beta + \gamma Q_F + \varepsilon, \qquad (4)$$

where

Q_H is a $T \times 1$ vector of yearly export flows;

X a $T \times K$ matrix of variables that enter into the determination of Q_H;

β a $K \times 1$ coefficient vector;

Q_F a $T \times 1$ vector of yearly foreign subsidiary production levels;

ε an unobserved $T \times 1$ error vector that includes, among other things, the influence of variables which have been omitted from the X matrix.

If all of the important determinants of export flows were included in the X matrix in appropriately chosen functional forms, the explanatory power of the foreign production variable in equation (4) would be nil and the regression equation should produce an estimate of γ close to zero. Such a zero coefficient is, as we shall indicate below, entirely consistent with either large negative or positive values of $-(\partial Q_H^* / \partial \tilde{Q}_F^*)$, our measure of the substitutability of home for foreign production.

[10] During the late sixties, the Office of Foreign Direct Investment was established for the purpose of monitoring cash outflows from U.S. parents to foreign subsidiaries. Given that a great percentage of subsidiary financing was generated overseas, it would be difficult to argue that the limited activities of OFDI constituted any real barrier to subsidiary expansion.

If, as is more likely to be the case, important explanatory variables are excluded from the X matrix, a slightly different picture emerges. If the omitted variables happen to be ones which also influence the optimal foreign production level—and given the simultaneous nature of the way in which Q_H^* and Q_F^* are determined it is difficult to envision variables which do not fit this description—then the foreign production variable will act as a surrogate for these omitted variables in the regression function. If the net impact of the omitted variables on foreign production is in the same direction as the net impact of these variables on exports, we should expect to observe a positive estimate of the coefficient γ. For example, if an important foreign market demand variable, such as income level, were omitted from X, the positive effect of income on Q_F^* would, in the absence of offsetting effects on Q_F^* of other omitted variables, act to establish a positive partial association between exports and subsidiary sales in the regression equation (4).

If, on the other hand, the omitted variable impacts in conflicting directions on foreign and domestic investment—as would, for example, be the case if a measure of relative unit-labor costs, foreign to domestic, were excluded from the X matrix—the effect would be to produce a negative coefficient γ.

In the case of Horst's industry cross-section regressions, the positive association between U.S. exports and foreign subsidiary sales may be accorded a similar interpretation. Despite the considerable care taken by Horst to control for important factors which might influence a firm's propensity to export from the United States, one is left with the feeling that many unmeasured characteristics of firms—the quality and aggressiveness of its management, the effectiveness of its product development efforts—play major roles in the determination of both the firm's level of exports and its volume of foreign affiliate sales. Horst's results indicate that firms with high level of foreign affiliate activity tend also to be firms with high levels of U.S. exports. They do not imply, in our judgment, that the level of U.S. exports would have been lower had the activities of foreign affiliates somehow been restrained. Likewise, given the importance of profits and liquidity variables in investment functions, and given the Tariff Commission finding that unit-labor costs in a preponderance of countries where DFI activities are concentrated are little different from those in the United States, one is not surprised to find that the Herring–Willett regressions also produce an apparent positive relationship between DFI and domestic investment.

The argument is essentially the same even if Q_H^* and Q_F^* are linked by a technological dependency, as when the subsidiary imports certain intermediate products from its U.S. parent. As a simple illustration, consider the case of an overseas subsidiary which requires $50 of intermediate inputs from its U.S. parent for each $100 in foreign sales. In the context of a growing foreign market one would expect to observe for such a subsidiary a positive association between series on subsidiary sales and U.S. exports to the subsidiary. This positive association clearly does not imply, however, that U.S. exports to the subsidiary host country would decline if subsidiary operations were suddenly prohibited. If U.S. production costs were not much higher than foreign costs and if foreign demand were not highly elastic, U.S. exports could almost double in the event of such a restriction.

An otherwise careful study that clearly illustrates a very similar methodological problem is one by Edward Ray (1977). Ray employs a simple model of a multinational firm engaged in four activities: (1) production at home; (2) production abroad; (3) sales at home; and (4) sales abroad. Only three of these activities are independent because of the constraint that total production and total sales in the two markets must balance. *Unless otherwise constrained*, an optimizing firm will thus maximize its profits by determining appropriate levels for any three of the four activities.

While for the firm the choice of the three activities is completely arbitrary, certain choices are more convenient for analysis than others. If, for example, the goal is to explore the relationship between foreign investment and domestic employment, the selection of domestic and foreign production levels as two of the activities would appear natural. The Ray study, however, performs the optimization process over *only* these two activities. The third activity, which in Ray's formulation is net exports (the difference between domestic production and sales), is not allowed to enter the optimization process at all, but is treated instead as an exogenous constraint variable. The result is the spurious appearance of exports in a final reduced form equation that is subsequently used for statistical estimation. Under the circumstances, the positive coefficient that Ray estimates for this variable simply does not support his inference that foreign investments are defensive in nature.

In evaluating the results of econometric studies of MNC behavior, the crucial point for our purposes is that a positive association between foreign and domestic activity variables (or a zero or negative association, for that matter) implies virtually nothing about what would have happened had firms been kept from investing abroad. Econometric studies which measure the statistical association between domestic and foreign activity variables may provide a basis for summarizing various potentially interesting relationships involved in the foreign investment phenomenon but contribute very little useful information on which to base judgments about the degree of substitutability of home for foreign production. In the next chapter, therefore, we consider an alternative strategy for approaching the "what would have happened otherwise?" question.

Chapter III

Measurement of Home–Foreign Substitution

This chapter has a threefold purpose. First, we briefly outline the role of several key factors that influence the degree of home–foreign substitution in models of foreign investment. Next, we develop a simplified prototype model of a multinational firm, which we employ to construct a closed form expression for the home–foreign substitution parameter. Finally, we indicate how one might go about estimating the magnitude of this parameter with the crude information currently available and indicate the priority areas in which better data would be required for superior future estimations.

Factors Affecting Home–Foreign Substitution

In order to determine the degree of substitution between home and foreign investment, our general approach will be to compare the level of domestic employment in the hypothetical MNC under two polar policy regimes—namely, regimes with and without the option of

27

foreign production. Within this framework, the foreign investment process involves the allocation of mobile capital resources over two (or possibly more) production sites, with the amounts of factor inputs and outputs determined by the criterion of global profit maximization.

Even this simple mode of analysis raises some very basic questions about the nature of the DFI process and how we view capital mobility in particular. The simple profit-maximization model outlined above operates as if the MNC controls a fixed amount of physical capital which it can distribute over various production sites according to the local rate of return. It is obvious, however, that in most cases the MNCs stock of real capital—that is, its property, plant, and equipment— cannot be unbolted, disassembled, and moved across international borders. This framework is a convenient fiction that allows us to bypass financial aspects of foreign investment and deal with real quantities only. It also has imbedded in it a particular view of how real and financial variables in the firm are connected.[1]

We assume here that firms seek out the cheapest source of supply for loanable funds. These funds are then used for the purchase of capital goods until the internal rate of return in each site is set equal to the borrowing rate. Although neither capital goods currently in place nor their services are sold directly in international markets, *new* capital goods are traded in a market that is sufficiently broad that international prices and intrafirm returns are roughly equalized. Although these convenient underlying assumptions will be common to all of our later models, we recognize that they are by no means appropriate for all cases. For example, it is quite possible that both borrowing rates and internal rates of return on investments could differ within a multinational firm, especially if overseas investments are required to be financed out of local sources. Likewise, there are many circumstances in which international prices for fixed capital inputs will not be exactly equalized.

The specification of production relationships within the firm is also of fundamental importance. Assumptions regarding the number of distinct factors of production and stages of processing, the degree

---

[1] A similarly simplified framework is usually applied in macroeconomic, general equilibrium analyses of foreign investment, such as that in Kemp (1969). The analogy between micro and macro models in this area is considered in greater detail in Horst (1973) and Rodriguez (1975).

of factor substitution, and the possible presence of scale economies, externalities, and joint products will have direct implications for the measure of home–foreign substitution that is derived from our model. For example, it is sometimes claimed that DFI allows the international firm to achieve economies of scale sufficient to more than make up for any jobs displaced in the initial transfer, or that foreign operations serve to increase domestic output and employment through favorable backward or forward linkages within the multinational firm itself. Both of these arguments clearly turn on specific assumptions about the nature of the firm's production relationships. Similarly, to determine the effect of foreign investment on employment within specific skill categories, it will be necessary to disaggregate employment and indicate the degree of substitution between various skill classes. In the prototype cases given below, however, we shall limit ourselves to an elementary specification of production technology—i.e., fixed coefficients, two factors of production in addition to capital (labor and material inputs), and constant or decreasing returns to scale.

Another important consideration is the degree to which production technology differs between the home and foreign location. (The term "production technology" is used in a broad sense to encompass both differences in productivity and choice of technique.) Until recently, the conventional view of direct foreign investment was that it represented a response to special local factors, such as climate or natural resources. By locating in the foreign site the firm was thereby able to realize a special advantage previously unavailable to it. Accordingly, production techniques and conventional measures of productivity could be assumed to differ sharply between foreign and comparable home operations.

Although this characterization may still be appropriate for certain types of investment, such as those in raw material extraction, the motivation is markedly different for a wide class of foreign investments. It is argued by many observers of recent U.S. DFI that its objective is not so much to take advantage of local technological factors but rather to export firm-specific or industry-specific technology to a new location.[2] Thus, much of recent U.S. investment activity—particularly

---

[2] Kindleberger and Hymer were early proponents of this view; see, for example, Hymer (1960) and Kindleberger (1969). An excellent survey of this point and related issues is found in Hufbauer (1975). See also Magee (1976) for related theoretical discussion.

overseas investments in manufacturing in developed markets—is regarded as a mechanism whereby U.S. firms can further extend the market power implicit in their control over high-powered technology. According to this view, essentially the same production possibilities apply at home and abroad; furthermore, if factor costs are not greatly different, if substitution possibilities are narrow, or if MNCs are simply reluctant to explore alternative factor combinations, then techniques used overseas will be similar to those used at home.[3]

Having made this distinction, however, it is necessary to qualify it immediately by pointing out that technology transfer through foreign investment is not always costless and complete. On this point the current literature—particularly the literature on transfer of technology through MNCs to developing markets—is full of examples of the obstacles that may be encountered.[4] Thus, it is clear that in any model of the DFI process it will be essential to specify the degree to which the firm is responding to local vis-à-vis firm-specific technological factors and the degree to which it is able to export its technology to a foreign site. Since our focus is on DFI in manufacturing, in the simple models developed below we shall assume that DFI is of the "modern" type and that investing firms use identical technologies at home and abroad.

Another important ingredient in our foreign investment model will be specific assumptions about the structure of both product and factor markets. On the product demand side a basic distinction must be made between perfectly competitive and imperfectly competitive cases—i.e., between markets where the firm faces an infinitely elastic demand and those with a finitely elastic demand curve. (In addition, once we attribute some monopoly power to the firm, we also have to specify whether or not it is able to discriminate between sales in home and foreign markets.) Although in some instances it may be correct to assume perfect competition, it is probably more appropriate to assume that the demand curves for the representative firm are less

---

[3] Some evidence has accumulated that multinational firms do indeed tend to replicate the domestic technology in overseas foreign sites, with the principal adjustment being only a change in scale. See, for example, Morley and Smith (1977a, b) and references therein.

[4] See, for example, Teece (1976) or Baranson (1970).

than infinitely elastic both at home and abroad. This monopoly power can be attributed to proprietary control over technology defined narrowly (i.e., patents, "lead time," specialized production skills, etc.), effective product differentiation, or efficient management—a view that is clearly consistent with the previous characterization of modern DFI. The presence of this monopoly power is strongly suggested by the large size of the typical MNC producer and the small number of firms in the international market for many products.

Similar issues can be raised on the factor supply side. It is well documented that foreign investment in some circumstances (particularly in cases of enclave-type investment) can have a significant impact on factor prices and factor supply in local markets. It will be assumed, however, primarily for simplicity of exposition, that these cases are the exception rather than the rule. Hence, in most of our examples we shall assume that the firm purchases its factor services in markets with a fixed supply price. It will be possible, however, for both the supply price and factor productivity to differ from country to country.

When the issue of oligopoly or monopoly is raised, it is also essential to specify firm strategy and firm optimizing behavior. Although it is recognized that a firm facing an oligopolistic market can adopt a number of possible strategies vis-à-vis its competitors, it will be convenient to assume that the firm takes its demand curve as given, and that the position of that curve is not influenced by the firm's own behavior. Hence, in the examples below the firm will be assumed to display the usual short-run profit maximizing behavior of the simple monopolist. We exclude by assumption such strategies as limit pricing, constant market share, or other behavior in which the firm attempts to control the position of its own demand curve.[5]

In addition to the factors mentioned above, the decision to invest abroad and the degree of substitution between home and foreign investment will be strongly influenced by any commercial policy in either country which causes prices in the home and foreign markets to diverge. Tariffs are the most familiar example—and the one which

---

[5] If, for example, under a simplified version of limit pricing the MNC were to set prices—and, thereby, output—at the margin which effectively bars entry by other firms, then any transfer of production back from overseas site (due, say, to restrictions on DFI) would imply a one-for-one increase in home output. In this case σ would be 1.0.

we shall use in the illustrations below—but it is clear that quotas, production taxes, consumption taxes, taxes on factor use, and other nontariff barriers to trade such as transport costs act in a similar fashion.[6]

Likewise, differential rates of taxation of firm income may affect not only the flow of funds within the MNC but also the location of production. For instance, if foreign rates of taxation are sufficiently low, the international firm may choose to produce even in a high-cost foreign production site. The possibility of differential rates of taxation also raises the issue of the use of artificial transfer prices to concentrate profits in the low tax jurisdiction.[7]

Finally, we should point out that this review of issues is by no means exhaustive, and is only intended to provide a framework for dealing with basic questions. Although we might well add such other factors as different attitudes toward risk, the short-run impact of exchange rate changes, and special financial and institutional constraints on foreign investment, we abstract from these issues for expositional convenience.

A Simple Model for Measuring Home–Foreign Substitution

Before considering the details of any particular model of direct foreign investment, it is important to make several preliminary observations on the outcomes these models are likely to produce. First, in a complete model, we should consider the possibility of both home and foreign production for both home and foreign sales. In such a model, there are four possible combinations of production and sales sites. However, if there are any significant international differences in costs—including transport costs and tariffs, in particular— at least one of these combinations ordinarily is eliminated. Put another way, it is unlikely that a stable equilibrium can be produced in which there occur *both* home production for the foreign market *and* foreign production for the home market; depending on the structure of prices and costs, one of these cross-hauling outcomes must be noncompetitive.

---

[6] There is by now a very large empirical and theoretical literature on the issue of the effect of both taxes and tariffs on foreign investment. A survey and references can be found in Hufbauer (1975).

[7] This case has been discussed extensively by Horst (1971).

In most of the discussion below we shall assume that the foreign production–home sales option is not viable and will be dropped; it will be apparent that following the other option (i.e., deleting the home production–foreign sales case) produces a parallel analysis. Thus, in our most general case we shall be left with the possibility of home production for either home or foreign sales, and foreign production for foreign sales. Also, in this first analysis it will be convenient to think of both foreign sales and production taking place in a single overseas site, although this is obviously not the case for many MNCs.

Second, we shall confine our attention to cases that produce determinate solutions. It is well known, for example, that if a firm faces a perfectly elastic demand curve and constant production costs, it is not possible to determine the profit-maximizing level of output by the usual techniques, unless some additional relevant information is supplied. The firm can produce an indefinite amount of product for a positive profit on each unit (or it suffers a loss on each unit and will produce none at all). Although there may be some short-run examples of this type of behavior, in the slightly longer run any such firm will capture a significant share of its market, and its demand curve will take on some finite elasticity. Since it is necessary to introduce some constraint on the firm to obtain deterministic outcomes, we shall assume that the typical foreign-investing firm has already explored these opportunities and reached the point at which it faces a declining demand curve.[8]

Finally, since considerable attention has been paid to this point the literature,[9] it may be worthwhile to distinguish cases according to whether or not they produce "interior" solutions. In this context the interior solution is one in which, even with the foreign investment option, the MNC still produces at home some part of its output for foreign sales. The analysis of these so-called "interior" cases is considerably more complex, since any change in conditions affecting the foreign market will have some additional indirect implications for home production through this joint-supply aspect. Some models with interior solutions are discussed briefly in the next chapter; for the model we consider immediately below, however, this is not a relevant issue.

[8] This assumption is also consistent with our description of the modern DFI process.

[9] See, for example, Horst (1971) or Adler and Stevens, (1974).

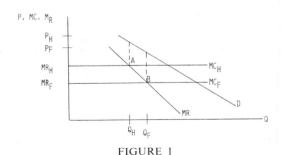

FIGURE 1

A very simple model that illustrates the essential ingredients for an estimation of the home–foreign substitution effect is shown in Fig. 1.

The demand curve for sales in the foreign market facing the potential foreign investor is given by D; the corresponding marginal revenue curve is shown as MR. This diagram is drawn on the assumption that all relevant production by the MNC is for foreign sale; the technical analysis is made considerably more involved by the introduction of a home market for MNC product—although the qualitative results of the analysis are not greatly altered. Production both at home and abroad is assumed to be carried out under constant marginal costs, indicated by MC_H and MC_F, respectively. Labor–output ratios are taken to be constant. In accordance with our earlier characterization of the technology transfer process they are also assumed to be identical in foreign and home production. Consequently, if we temporarily ignore any costs not directly related to production, such as transport charges and tariffs, the different levels of the two MC curves can be attributed to local cost differences—in this model primarily differences in labor costs.

Figure 1 assumes that foreign wages are lower than domestic wages.[10] If the MNC is required to serve the foreign market exclusively through home production and export, it will produce at point A at which home marginal cost equals marginal revenue. The equilibrium product price will be established at P_H; quantity Q_H will be produced and sold in the foreign market. Alternatively, if the constraint on foreign production is eliminated, the firm will choose to produce all

---

[10] It should be obvious that differences in local nonlabor costs or in productivity will have an analogous effect on the cost curves of Fig. 1.

output abroad at point B in the diagram. Price will be reduced to P_F and output and sales will increase to Q_F. Since the labor–output ratio is fixed, for this case a direct measure of the number of home man-hours of employment lost (in the opportunity cost sense) per man-hour of foreign employment is

$$\sigma = \frac{L_H}{L_F} = \frac{Q_H l}{Q_F l} = \frac{Q_H}{Q_F}, \qquad (1)$$

where L_H and L_F are employment levels corresponding to Q_H and Q_F, respectively, and l is the firm's technical labor–output ratio. Although Q_F is observable, ordinarily the determination of Q_H is somewhat involved and requires a considerable amount of detailed information about both demand and cost conditions. However, with a few additional simplifying assumptions Q_H and, thus, measures of σ, can be inferred directly from readily available information.

We shall assume that over the range of price and quantities shown in Fig. 1 the elasticity of the demand curve facing the firm is approximately constant.[11] That is, we shall assume that

$$Q = Q(P) = \frac{N}{P^\eta}, \qquad (2)$$

where N is an arbitrary scale factor, and η is the constant elasticity of demand, defined by $\eta = -(dQ/dP) \cdot (P/Q)$. This means that the corresponding marginal revenue curve must have the form

$$\mathrm{MR} = P \cdot \left(1 - \frac{1}{\eta}\right) = \left(\frac{N}{Q}\right)^{1/\eta} \cdot \left(\frac{\eta - 1}{\eta}\right). \qquad (3)$$

---

[11] The demand curve facing the firm in Fig. 1 reflects all relevant influences on demand, including entry by other potential competitors, etc. A point elasticity estimate will capture these effects in a small neighborhood, but care must be exercised in extrapolating beyond the point in question. If the range of cost differences is narrow, however, this may not be a serious source of error. In addition, it should be pointed out that this specification does not allow for shifts in demand (and shifts in demand for related products) that are occasioned by the establishment of a foreign subsidiary. There is some evidence that "externalities" of this type may be important, particularly in consumer-oriented industries where local product identification and effective distribution are significant factors. Since effects of this type cannot be inferred retrospectively from subsidiary income sheet information, we are forced to ignore this issue here; by this omission we may somewhat overestimate the net job loss associated with DFI. For more information on this issue, see Horst (1974, 1976), Lipsey and Weiss (1976a, b).

Since at the profit-maximizing points, A and B, marginal (and average) costs will be set equal to marginal revenue, from (3) one can readily obtain

$$\sigma = \frac{Q_H}{Q_F} = \left(\frac{MC_F}{MC_H}\right)^{\eta}. \tag{4}$$

Several important aspects of this simple relationship deserve to be pointed out. First, in this case our measure of σ depends *only* on relative costs and the elasticity of demand. Since η measures the degree of market competitiveness, substitution between home and foreign production will be high when η is absolutely low, as one would expect. The value of σ will also be high when there is only a small difference in relative costs between home and foreign sites. It is also worth pointing out that the degree of substitution is independent of the arbitrary scale parameter, N.

Finally, one can infer the elasticity of demand from the following relationship, based on equation (3):

$$\eta = \frac{(P/MC_F)}{(P/MC_F) - 1}. \tag{5}$$

For our constant marginal cost case this can be recast in the convenient form

$$\eta = \frac{(R/V)}{(R/V) - 1} = \frac{R}{R - V}, \tag{6}$$

where R is total revenue (from foreign subsidiary sales) and V is the corresponding level of total variable costs. Thus, in order to estimate the degree of home–foreign substitution one only needs information about relative cost differences and the markup ratio in the foreign subsidiary.

As we demonstrate in Chapter IV, this extremely useful result can be readily extended to more complex cases with relatively minor modifications. However, since the assumptions regarding both constant costs and less than perfectly elastic demand seem quite plausible for the typical foreign investing firm, even in the simple form shown in equations (4) and (6), one can obtain a useful measure of the degree of substitution between home and foreign production. Furthermore,

the effect of ad valorem tariffs and transport costs can be easily integrated into the analysis by incorporating them into the level of home
unit costs. For example, if we use t to represent the ad valorem percentage tariff plus transport cost, we need only rewrite equation (4)
as[12]

$$\sigma = \frac{Q_H}{Q_F} = \left(\frac{MC_F}{MC_H(1 + t)}\right)^\eta.$$ (7)

From Fig. 1 it can be seen immediately that in this case high tariffs and
transport costs will tend to reduce the value of σ.[12]

Based on (7), we have employed existing data in the construction of
numerical estimates of the home–foreign substitution parameters for
major manufacturing industries. The results of these computations
(the details and data sources for which are described in Appendix A)
are summarized in Table 1.

---

[12] Ideally the factor $1 + t$ ought to be a measure of the effective rate of protection
that includes not only tariffs on intermediate inputs but also the tariff equivalent of
various nontariff barriers, such as quotas, government preferences, domestic taxes, etc.
Our sample calculations below use tariff values for final products only. Ignoring tariffs
on intermediate products is probably not too damaging to our immediate objective here,
since the scale and relative ranking of protection levels is not likely to be greatly affected.
The implication of not specifically including nontariff barriers is less certain, but recent
studies of nontariff barriers to U.S. exports (Baldwin, 1970; U.S. Tariff Commission,
1973 indicate that they are most frequently applied to the export of agricultural and
animal products, coal, petroleum, and textiles. With the exception of the latter, exports
forgone due to DFI are likely to have a relatively minor impact on the substitution
effect that we calculate. Nevertheless, it should be apparent that the measures of protection we use must be taken only as indicative of the overall level of protection.

In addition, one special circumstance deserves mention. In some instances host
countries have made the establishment of local facilities a prerequisite for export from
the United States. In such instances, of course, a ban on foreign subsidiary production
will not stimulate export production in the United States at all; for firms operating under
constraints of this type, sigma is effectively zero. Failure to treat this problem explicitly
probably introduces errors of only second-order importance, since the lion's share of
activity on which the estimates in Table 1 are based is concentrated in Canada and
Europe, where import restrictions are considerably less common than in developing
countries. Specific quantitative evidence on the importance of trade restrictions in the
decision to invest abroad is conspicuously lacking, however, and this issue should receive
much more careful attention in future data collection and empirical work.

TABLE 1

Calculation of σ for major manufacturing industries

Industry name	(1) $\dfrac{MC_F}{MC_H}$	(2) η	(3) t	(4) σ	(5) σ^a	(6) σ^b
Food	0.918	3.41	0.230	0.368	0.462	0.237
Chemicals	0.898	2.75	0.200	0.441	0.545	0.314
Primary and fabricated metals	0.885	4.87	0.173	0.245	0.341	0.131
Electrical machinery	0.836	2.86	0.214	0.345	0.418	0.237
Nonelectrical machines	0.836	2.86	0.196	0.358	0.438	0.247
Transportation equipment	0.886	5.51	0.198	0.191	0.277	0.091
Rubber	0.867	2.58	0.167	0.463	0.556	0.325
Paper	0.867	2.58	0.167	0.463	0.556	0.325
Other manufacturing	0.867	2.58	0.233	0.402	0.480	0.289

[a] Based on transport costs = 0.05 × value of shipments.
[b] Based on transport costs = 0.30 × value of shipments.

While most of the ingredients used in our calculation of σ are inexact, the reliability of the tariff and transport cost entries is especially questionable. For this reason, we have calculated a range of values of σ by allowing transport costs to vary between 5 % and 30 % of the value of shipments (variations in transport and tariff costs produce, in our model, equivalent variations in sigma). The data and procedures employed for estimating elasticity values were also somewhat crude, but on the whole, the figures in column (2) of Table 1 appear entirely consistent with the characterization of the MNC as a large, oligopolistic enterprise.

Column (4) of Table 1, our best estimates of sigma, range from 0.191 for the transportation equipment industry to 0.463 for the paper and rubber industries. Recalling that σ represents the fraction of foreign markets which could have been served by exporting from the United States, these figures provide a measure of support for the business community's claim that foreign production operations are largely defensive in nature. Even our upperbound estimates of σ (column (5) of Table 1) appear quite consistent with the assertion that the alternative to overseas production would be a very large-scale erosion of the foreign markets now served by U.S. MNCs.

Numerous qualifying remarks to the substitution parameter estimates of Table 1 could be discussed at this point, all of which reduce to a statement that our estimates must be regarded as extremely tentative in character. As inexact as these estimates may be, however, they do represent an attempt to assess home-foreign substitution by applying available data within received models of firm behavior; as such, they stand in contrast to previous efforts in this area in which judgments about substitution have been based either purely on assumption or on inferences drawn from improperly specified econometric models.

Chapter IV

Micro Model Extensions

This chapter is a brief side excursion in which we extend the highly simplified model of the previous chapter to somewhat more complex cases. The spirit of the analysis is similar in that we seek to determine expressions for the home–foreign substitution parameter that are capable of direct estimation on the basis of very limited information, using the general techniques outlined in Chapter III.[1] We make the same assumptions as before—i.e., profit maximization, monopoly power in final product markets, and identical technology in domestic and foreign sites.

Variable Unit Costs, Foreign Sales Only

The first modification of the basic model involves replacing the constant marginal cost curves of Fig. 1 from Chapter III with non-constant cost curves, as shown in Fig. 1. The origin of the foreign

---

[1] The reader is invited to compare the analysis in this chapter to that in Adler and Stevens (1974), Horst (1971), or Horst (1973), which use microeconomic models to analyze multinational firm behavior but where the emphasis is slightly different.

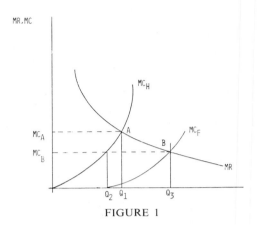

FIGURE 1

marginal cost curve has been placed in the diagram so that, when foreign production is allowed and marginal revenue is set equal to marginal cost in each site, the horizontal sum of the curves measures the total output of the MNC in the two locations. We still assume that all relevant sales take place in the foreign market; hence, MR is still the marginal revenue curve associated with the MNCs foreign demand curve.

As it is drawn, Fig. 1 is an illustration of an "interior solution" case in which, even when foreign investment is allowed, cost conditions are such that the MNC continues to produce at home some part of its output for foreign sale. When DFI is not allowed, quantity Q_1 will be produced at home for export; when DFI is allowed, quantity Q_2 will be produced at home and $Q_3 - Q_2$ will be produced abroad. Hence, in this case the corresponding measure for the substitution parameter, σ, is

$$\sigma = \frac{Q_1 - Q_2}{Q_3 - Q_2}. \tag{1}$$

Although in principle a closed form expression for Q_1, Q_2, Q_3, and σ could be obtained from information about cost curves, in practice this calculation would be rather involved for most cases. For at least one case, however, the analysis is straightforward and yields some useful insights.

We shall assume that cost structures are such that the elasticity of output with respect to marginal cost is constant. (Under conditions of perfect competition in factor markets this is equivalent to assuming constant elasticity of supply). Thus, we can write

$$Q_F = Z_F(MC_F)^{\varepsilon_F} \quad \text{and} \quad \varepsilon_F = \frac{dQ_F}{dMC_F} \cdot \frac{MC_F}{Q_F}, \tag{2a}$$

$$Q_H = Z_H(MC_H)^{\varepsilon_H} \quad \text{and} \quad \varepsilon_H = \frac{dQ_H}{dMC_H} \cdot \frac{MC_H}{Q_H}, \tag{2b}$$

where ε_F and ε_H are constant supply elasticities and Z_F and Z_H are scale parameters for foreign and home costs, respectively—a formulation which is appropriate, for example, when both factor supply prices and returns to scale within the firm are nonvarying. Under these circumstances the values of ε_H and ε_F are determined by production technology alone; differences in local factor costs affect only the scale parameters, Z_H and Z_F. When the same technology is used at home and abroad, we can simplify the notation by writing $\varepsilon_H = \varepsilon_F = \varepsilon$.

We show in Appendix B that, under these assumptions, profit maximization implies that

$$\sigma = \frac{1}{\mu}\left[(1 + \mu)^{\varepsilon/(\varepsilon + \eta)} - 1\right], \tag{3}$$

when μ is a production-share measure defined by

$$\mu \equiv \left(\frac{Q_F}{Q_H}\right)_B, \tag{4}$$

and where the subscript B indicates values taken at point B in Fig. 1. It can be seen by inspection that σ in (3) ordinarily must lie in the range $0 < \sigma < 1.0$; also, σ will normally be higher when ε is large, when η is small, and when μ is small. Estimates of μ for this case could be obtained by direct observation; estimates of η can be derived from equation (1) in Chapter III by procedures similar to those described earlier. Calculations of the supply elasticity ε require information primarily on returns to scale within the firm. An important point is that neither the absolute level of unit costs nor relative unit costs appear in (3) above—a feature that greatly facilitates estimation. Hence, if information on returns to scale is available and the implied supply elasticity is not large, an estimate of σ can be obtained quite readily. If returns to scale are constant, and the supply elasticity is large, then the equations from the simpler model in Chapter III may be used instead.

Since in this case the equilibrium at point B is an interior equilibrium, when we add tariffs and other similar ad valorem charges to home production costs, the analysis becomes considerably more complex than that of Chapter III. The additional complexity arises because under any change in production or demand conditions, profit-maximization will now imply shifts in production in *both* sites. This effect can be seen by noticing that when the firm maximizes its total profits,

$$\Pi = \Pi_H + \Pi_F,$$

where

$$\Pi_H = \frac{P}{1 + t} Q_H - C_H(Q_H) \quad \text{and} \quad \Pi_F = PQ_F - C_F(Q_F)$$

are profits from home production and foreign production respectively, it is the net price facing home producers, $P/(1 + t)$, that enters into the calculation of home revenue. The profit maximizing conditions for this case are now

$$MC_H = \frac{MR}{1 + t} - \left[\left(\frac{P}{\eta} \right) \left(\frac{\mu}{1 + \mu} \right) \left(\frac{t}{1 + t} \right) \right], \tag{5a}$$

$$MC_F = MR + \left[\left(\frac{P}{\eta} \right) \left(\frac{1}{1 + \mu} \right) \left(\frac{t}{1 + t} \right) \right], \tag{5b}$$

and it is apparent that the level of the tariff will affect the allocation of production between home and foreign sites. Its level will also influence any inference we make about home–foreign substitution. The value of σ in this case can be expressed by

$$\sigma = \frac{Q_{H_A} - Q_{H_B}}{Q_{F_B}} = \frac{1}{\mu} \left[\left[\frac{MC_{H_A}}{MC_{H_B}} \right]^{\varepsilon} - 1 \right]. \tag{6}$$

The subscripts refer to values at point A (the no-DFI equilibrium point) and point B (the interior equilibrium point) in Fig. 1. We show in Appendix B that

$$\frac{MC_{H_A}}{MC_{H_B}} = \frac{(1 + \mu)^{(1 + \eta)/(\varepsilon + \eta)}}{(1 + \mu - T\mu)^{\eta/(\varepsilon + \eta)}}, \tag{7}$$

and hence, that

$$\sigma = \frac{1}{\mu} \left[\frac{(1 + \mu)^{(\varepsilon + \varepsilon\eta)/(\eta + \varepsilon)}}{(1 + \mu - T\mu)^{\varepsilon\eta/(\eta + \varepsilon)}} - 1 \right], \tag{8}$$

where the tariff parameter, T, is defined by

$$T = \frac{t}{\eta - 1}.$$

Equation (8) should be compared to equation (3). For small values of t, T also becomes small, and σ approaches the expression in (3). On the other hand, when tariffs are high, the value of σ will be high as well. The realization of a given home production share of sales in the face of high tariffs implies a greater foregone domestic output.

A similar result is encountered if we introduce differential rates of home and foreign taxation of profits into the model. In previous, noninterior cases the profit-maximizing equilibrium output, and hence σ, was unaffected by the level of taxation in the two countries. In interior cases, however, because of the joint-supply aspect of production, differential rates of taxation will affect output in *both* locations. As a result, tax levels will also influence the value of our measure of substitution.

When taxes are included in the model,[2] the profit-maximizing conditions become

$$MC_H = MR - \left[\left(\frac{t_H - t_F}{1 - t_H} \right) \left(\frac{P}{\eta} \right) \left(\frac{\mu}{1 + \mu} \right) \right], \tag{9a}$$

$$MC_F = MR + \left[\left(\frac{t_H - t_F}{1 - t_F} \right) \left(\frac{P}{\eta} \right) \left(\frac{1}{1 + \mu} \right) \right], \tag{9b}$$

where t_H and t_F represent the percentage rate of taxation of home and foreign profits, respectively. The marginal cost ratio now becomes

$$\frac{MC_{H_A}}{MC_{H_B}} = \frac{(1 + \mu)^{(1 + \eta)/(\varepsilon + \eta)}}{(1 + \mu - G\mu)^{\eta/(\varepsilon + \eta)}}, \tag{10}$$

---

[2] In this example we return to assuming that there are no tariffs or similar charges on products produced in the home site.

where the tax parameter, G, is defined by

$$G = \left(\frac{t_H - t_F}{1 - t_H}\right)\left(\frac{1}{\eta - 1}\right).$$

The expression for σ is therefore

$$\sigma = \frac{1}{\mu}\left[\frac{(1 + \mu)^{(\varepsilon + \varepsilon\eta)/(\varepsilon + \eta)}}{(1 + \mu - G\mu)^{\varepsilon\eta/(\varepsilon + \eta)}} - 1\right]. \tag{11}$$

It can be seen immediately from (11) that high home taxes (i.e., home taxes higher than foreign taxes) will have an effect that is parallel to that of tariffs in the previous example. *Ceteris paribus*, the level of foregone home production that we infer from any observed distribution of production between home and foreign sites will be higher, and, consequently, so will be our measure of σ.

Under current U.S. tax laws foreign-earned corporate income is required to be taxed at the same rate as domestic income with a full credit allowed for foreign taxes paid. If actual rates paid reflect this, the value of G in (11) would become zero and (11) would revert to the simpler expression in (3). If, however, the effective rate of total taxation on foreign earned income is believed to be less—say, due the use of deferrals and other exceptions—then the level of taxation on home income will exceed that on foreign income and the degree of substitution inferred from (11) should be increased. Put differently, to the extent that foreign investment is favored by the current structure of taxes, the elimination of the DFI option would bring about a larger increase in domestic activity than in the case in which taxes had a neutral effect.

Home Sales Included

In this case we relax the assumption maintained above that only foreign sales are relevant to the firm's production decision; we shall assume that the MNC serves *both* the home and foreign market. For simplicity we shall also revert to our earlier assumption that production in both locations is carried out under constant average costs. It will be apparent that the refinements of the previous cases can easily be grafted on to our results from this case.

When there are two markets for the MNCs output, the equilibrium pattern will be strongly affected by the firm's ability to separate sales in the two markets. First, assuming that the markets can be fully separated, the profit maximizing condition is that marginal cost be set equal to marginal revenue in each market, i.e.,

$$MC_H = MR_H = MR_F, \tag{12a}$$

$$MC_F = MR_H = MR_F. \tag{12b}$$

In terms of our earlier diagrams this means that we can simply reinterpret the marginal revenue curve in Fig. 1 of Chapter III as the horizontal sum of the marginal revenue curves from the home and foreign market. We show in Appendix B that our measure of σ is now given by

$$\sigma = \frac{Q_{H_A} - Q_{H_B}}{Q_{F_B}}.$$

We show in Appendix B that this is now equivalent to

$$\sigma = \frac{1}{1 + \theta} \left(\frac{MC_F}{MC_H}\right)^{\eta_H} + \frac{\theta}{1 + \theta} \left(\frac{MC_F}{MC_H}\right)^{\eta_F}, \tag{13}$$

where θ is a market share parameter that expresses the ratio of total sales in the foreign market to total sales in the home market at point B. Since sales at point B can be measured by direct observation, σ can be determined from information on relative costs and demand elasticities in the same way as was done in Chapter III.

If, on the other hand, the firm is *not* able to separate the two markets, the determination of σ is somewhat more involved and requires additional information. Here σ is given by

$$\sigma = \left[\frac{1}{1 + \theta} \cdot \left(\frac{P_B}{P_A}\right)^{\eta_H}\right] + \left[\frac{\theta}{1 + \theta} \cdot \left(\frac{P_B}{P_A}\right)^{\eta_F}\right]. \tag{14}$$

Although P_A cannot be observed directly, it can be inferred from information on marginal costs and the following relationship:

$$\left[\left(1 - \frac{1}{\eta_F}\right) - \frac{MC_H}{P_A}\right]\left[\left(1 - \frac{1}{\eta_H}\right) - \frac{MC_H}{P_A}\right] = \frac{1}{\eta_F \eta_H}. \tag{15}$$

Even in the extensions of the model we discuss in this chapter, we are still working with a greatly simplified version of a multinational firm. There are a number of additional refinements that invite inclusion in the analysis—the treatment of multiperiod cases, multiproduct technologies, and financial aspects such as joint ownership and the use of multiple currencies—all of which would move the model in the direction of greater realism. Moreover, the implications of particular strong assumptions about the shape of cost and demand curves should at some point be explored in depth.

The relatively simple cases that we have illustrated above suggest the direction in which the analysis might proceed, but the progression of results so far is a warning that a fully developed model would surely be complex. Obtaining a closed form expression for the substitution parameter in a considerably more general model would at best be very difficult. More complex models also promise to vastly oustrip the limited data resources that are currently available. All of this points to the pressing need for more extensive, timely, and reliable data collection in this area.

Chapter V

The Employment Impact of Direct Foreign Investment

In this chapter we illustrate a technique for estimating the changes in short-run employment that result from direct foreign investment. We deal explicitly with the home–foreign substitution effects discussed in the previous section and also with any possible offsets derived from DFI-related exports. In addition, we distinguish both direct and indirect employment effects, using an input–output table for U.S. industries. That is, we examine not only the immediate employment impact implied by a shift of production to foreign subsidiaries, but also the additional employment effect associated with changes in each sector as intermediate inputs adjust to the initial displacement of production. Although most writers on this subject have ignored these indirect effects, it is apparent that they can be extremely important,[1]

[1] A related paper that does not take these effects into account is Hawkins (1972b). Their importance has been emphasized in a large number of studies; for an illustration see Alterman (1965). As we shall show below, the indirect effects can outweigh the direct effects by a factor of as much as ten to one in those sectors with relatively low DFI which also provide substantial inputs to other sectors.

particularly in those cases in which production in foreign subsidiaries stimulates substantial home production of intermediate goods for export.

The Basic Input–Output Calculation

The primary employment effect of a given year's direct foreign investment, which we refer to as the "export displacement effect," can be computed as

$$[\Delta L_1] = -[l][I - A]^{-1}[q][\sigma][\Delta F], \tag{1}$$

where

$[\Delta L_1]$ is an $n \times 1$ vector of jobs lost due to the export displacement effect of DFI in each industry;

$[l]$ is an $n \times n$ diagonal matrix in which the diagonal elements are labor-input to total-output ratios for each industry;

$[I - A]^{-1}$ is an $n \times n$ Leontief inverse matrix;

$[q]$ is an $n \times n$ diagonal matrix in which the diagonal elements are total-output-to-capital ratios for each industry;

$[\sigma]$ is an $n \times n$ diagonal matrix in which diagonal elements indicate the extent to which DFI-related production substitutes for domestic production (complete substitution when $\sigma_i = 1.0$; no substitution when $\sigma_i = 0$) in each industry, as explained above;

$[\Delta F]$ is an $n \times 1$ vector of DFI (property, plant, and equipment expenditure) in each industry.

It may also be useful to express this relationship as the sum of a direct and an indirect effect in order to compare it with other estimates that fail to consider the indirect demand for intermediate inputs

$$[\Delta L_1] = - \{\underbrace{[l][q][\sigma][\Delta F]}_{\text{direct}} + \underbrace{[l][(I - A)^{-1} - I][q][\sigma][\Delta F]}_{\text{indirect}}\}. \tag{1'}$$

To this primary export-displacement effect (defined as negative for job losses) we also add a secondary export-stimulation effect to reflect the extent to which foreign subsidiaries obtain intermediate inputs from U.S. suppliers. This is defined as

$$[\Delta L_2] = [l][[I - A]^{-1}[\chi] - [\chi]][q][\Delta F],\qquad (2)$$

where

$[\Delta L_2]$ is an $n \times 1$ vector of jobs gained due to the export stimulation effect of DFI;

$[\chi]$ is an $n \times n$ diagonal matrix in which the diagonal elements indicate the share of inputs obtained from U.S. suppliers.

Expressed in this form, this computation assumes that in any given industry the same proportion of each input is imported. When this assumption is not valid, the proper alternative calculation is

$$[\Delta L_2] = [l][[I - A]^{-1}[A \otimes \chi] - [A \otimes \chi]][q][\Delta F],$$

where $[\chi]$ is an $n \times n$ matrix in which χ_{ij} expresses the percentage of input i to industry j that is imported from the United States and where $[A \otimes \chi]$ is the Kronecker product of the A and χ matrices. Because of limitations in our data, however, in the calculations that follow it was necessary to use the more aggregated version shown in equation (2).

We should mention that in using equations (1) and (2) to compute the employment effect of a given annual vector of DFI we are relying on a number of strong assumptions about the structure of production both at home and abroad. To be specific, not only are we accepting the conventional assumption of input–output analysis that aggregate input coefficients are constant, but we also assume that the same input coefficients apply to home and foreign production alike. For much of overseas investment this assumption may be plausible, but there are cases in which substitution possibilities exist and input coefficients could therefore vary. In addition, implicit in equations (1) and (2) is the assumption that when DFI occurs the effect on output and employment can be computed by using the *average* capital–output ratio in each sector. This raises two possible problems. First, ideally we should like to substitute the marginal capital–output ratio in this calculation; the average capital–output ratio is at best an approximation. Second, in many cases DFI occurs only in a particular subsector or stage of processing within the broad industry classifications we have designated. When the subsector capital–output ratio varies from the industry average ratio, a similar inaccuracy is introduced. If DFI tends to respond systematically to differences in factor costs, this assumption could produce an underestimate of the effect of DFI on job loss. If, for example, foreign unit-labor costs are low, DFI would tend to occur in the labor-intensive subsectors of industries, implying a greater degree of job loss than we would measure using industry average values. It might be possible to account partially for this effect by using labor–output ratios derived from more detailed foreign subsidiary data than those that were available to us. Also, equations (1) and (2) do not take into account indirect employment effects associated with fixed capital requirements, only those associated with current inputs. Since most subsidiary fixed capital inputs for construction are obtained locally, the omission of fixed capital requirements from the computation most likely causes a slight underestimate of job displacement. Again, until more detailed information on both DFI and industry structure is available, we are forced to assume that average ratios can serve as suitable proxies and trust that the resulting bias is small.

Equations (1) and (2) account for the two main effects of DFI on domestic employment. There is, however, an additional modification that may be needed in some circumstances to allow for import substitution of subsidiary output for domestic production. First, notice that the export displacement effect, as specified in equation (1), applies equally to displacement of exports or domestic demand. Hence, import substitution effects in the first round are already fully accounted for by (1). However, if DFI is assumed to bring about a permanent change in the structure of domestic demand, an additional adjustment for subsequent rounds is needed. This adjustment can be made by changing the input–output coefficients in each column according to the additional percentage of total input requirements derived from DFI sources.

The most sensible approach is to attribute these extra imports to the "undistributed imports" row in the I–O matrix and reduce other rows correspondingly. Thus, in this case we should add to the vector of export displacement effects

$$[l][I - A]^{-1}[\gamma][q][\sigma][\Delta F], \tag{3}$$

and from the export stimulation effect we should subtract

$$[l][[I - A]^{-1}[\chi][\gamma] - [\chi][\gamma]][q][\Delta F], \tag{4}$$

where $[\gamma]$ is an $n \times n$ diagonal matrix in which γ_i expresses the additional percentage of good i obtained from external sources (subsidiaries) in each round.

As was the case in the export stimulation effect, this calculation assumes proportional changes in industry input coefficients. Where the assumption is inappropriate, the expressions for $[I - A]^{-1}[\chi][\gamma]$ in (3) and (4) should be modified to a Kronecker product expression as on page 51. When this γ effect is assumed to be small, the unadjusted measures shown in (1) and (2) are appropriate. In our computations below we performed tests both with γ equal to our best estimates of its historical value and with γ equal to zero; inclusion of nonzero γ turned out to have only a small effect on the results in most cases.

Data Sources and Preparation

Equations (1)–(4) indicate that the essential data inputs for computation are

(A) the $[I - A]^{-1}$ Leontief inverse matrix,
(B) corresponding capital–output and labor–output ratios,
(C) series on annual DFI, disaggregated by an industrial classification consistent with the above, and
(D) measures of σ, χ, and γ for each industrial sector.

For the Leontief inverse we used a revised version of the U.S. Department of Labor, Bureau of Labor Statistics, 129-sector, 1963 I–O table, updated to 1970. Comparable employment and constant-dollar capital stock figures were obtained from the same source. The degree of industry detail in these data was roughly at the SIC three-digit level. The U.S. Department of Commerce, Bureau of Economic Analysis, provided series on annual property, plant, and equipment expenditures (DFI) by their sample of roughly 500 multinational firms. These DFI data were disaggregated by industry to roughly a two and three-digit level and covered the eight years, 1966–1973.[2] Although a

---

[2] The DFI data are shown in Table 1 in Appendix C.

TABLE 1

Industry classifications for input–output calculations
(21-order industry classification)

21-order industry number	Industry name	OBE classification code	SIC equivalent
1	Agriculture, forestry, and fisheries	100	01, 07–09
2	Mining	200	101–106, 108, 109, 11, 12, 14
3	Petroleum	300	13
4	Food products	410	20
5	Paper and allied products	420	26
6	Chemicals and allied products	430	28
7	Rubber and miscellaneous plastic products (finished)	440	30
8	Primary and fabricated metals	450	33, 34
9	Machinery (except electrical)	460	35
10	Electrical machinery, equipment, and supplies	470	36
11	Transportation equipment	480	37
12	Other manufacturing	490	19, 22–25, 27, 31, 38, 39
13	Transportation, communication, and public utilities	500	40, 41, 42, 44, 45, 47, 48, 491–497
14	Trade	600	52–59, 501–504, 506, 508, 5014, 5052–5054, 5059, 5072, 5074, 5077, 5091, 5094–5097, 5099
15	Banking and insurance, and miscellaneous industries	700 800	60–64, 67, 15–17, 65, 66, 70, 72, 73, 78, 79
16	Post Office, Commodity Credit Corporation, and other federal enterprises	*a*	*a*
17	State and local government enterprises	*a*	*a*
18	Directly allocated imports	*a*	*a*
19	Transferred imports	*a*	*a*
20	Business travel, entertainment, and gifts	*a*	*a*
21	Office supplies	*a*	*a*

a Not comparable.

TABLE 2

Estimates of χ and γ used in 21-order matrix calculations[a]

Industry number	Industry name	χ	γ
1	Agriculture, forestry, and fisheries	0.0459	0.0005
2	Mining	0.1707	0.0089
3	Petroleum	0.0155	0.0414
4	Food products	0.2855	0.0032
5	Paper and allied products	0.0853	0.0088
6	Chemicals and allied products	0.0904	0.0074
7	Rubber and miscellaneous plastic products (finished)	0.2403	0.0088
8	Primary and fabricated metals	0.0787	0.0174
9	Machinery (except electrical)	0.1956	0.0091
10	Electrical machinery, equipment, and supplies	0.1660	0.0091
11	Transportation equipment	0.3767	0.0486
12	Other manufacturing	0.0782	0.0088
13	Transportation, communication, and public utilities	0.0696	0.0005
14	Trade	0.1521	0.0031
15	Banking and insurance, and miscellaneous industries	0.0601	0.0005

[a] For definitions and sources, see text.

considerable number of data points were deleted because of potential disclosure problems, continuous series could be constructed for 36 industry groups at the two- and three-digit level. The process whereby the industry definitions in (A), (B), and (C) were made conformable yielded a consistent 21-order classification scheme in which 15 sectors were I–O sectors. The industry and SIC content of this 21-order classification are shown in Table 1.

Since the data were taken from an annual sample, it was also necessary to convert them to constant 1963-dollar universe estimates. This conversion was made in several steps. Disaggregated universe estimates were available for 1966; also, for each year universe estimates were available for each of the 15 I–O sectors in the 21-order classification scheme for the same sample of firms.[3] To obtain universe estimates

---

[3] Universe estimates for 1966 were provided with the BEA data; aggregate annual universe estimates were taken from various issues of the *Survey of Current Business*.

for the more disaggregated 36-order scheme, we applied the 1966 sample to universe ratio for each 36-order subsector together with the 21-order subtotals for each year. Finally, we deflated all DFI data to 1963 constant-dollar figures using the corresponding value of the Department of Commerce nonresidential fixed investment deflator.

The procedures used for obtaining tentative estimates of σ have already been discussed in Chapter III.[4] Estimates of χ and γ were derived from data supplied in the Department of Commerce *Special Survey of U.S. Multinational Companies for* 1970 (*DOC Special Survey*). Estimates of χ were made by first finding the share of intermediate product obtained from the United States in total subsidiary sales and dividing that figure by the value of intermediate inputs to total activity for the corresponding industry in the input–output matrix. Values of γ were found by dividing subsidiary exports by total sales of home office reporters in the same industry.[5] Since the number of

---

[4] Values for σ in manufacturing sectors (4)–(12) were taken from Table 1 in Chapter III. Sigma values for sectors (1) Agriculture *et al.* (0.457) and (15) Banking *et al.* (0.457) were derived by procedures identical to those discussed in the Appendix A. For sectors (2) Mining and (3) Petroleum a zero value for σ was assigned because of the extremely low short-run supply elasticity in those sectors. This means that our study abstracts from any direct displacements in those sectors (although there may be indirect effects). Since zero is the minimum value for σ, we may slightly underestimate total job loss on this account.

[5] The numerator in the calculation of χ was formed by

$$\frac{X_1}{X_3 - X_2}$$

where

X_1 = U.S. exports to foreign subsidiaries for further processing, 1970 DOC Survey, p. 55, line 8.
X_2 = U.S. exports to foreign subsidiaries for resale, 1970 DOC Survey, p. 55, line 5.
X_3 = net sales of foreign subsidiaries, 1970 DOC Survey, p. 23, line 5.

The value of γ was calculated by

$$\frac{X_1}{X_2}$$

where

X_1 = subsidiary exports to U.S., 1970 DOC Survey, p. 23, line 19.
X_2 = net sales of U.S. respondents, 1970 DOC Survey, p. 19, line 9.

sectors in this survey was considerably less detailed than in our other information, we were forced to include several sectors in the "other industries" catagory. In spite of these limitations, however, the values for most manufacturing sectors could be computed directly. The figures used are shown in Table 2.

Calculation of Net Employment Effects

Since, the parameters σ, χ, and γ were probably the least reliable ingredients in our computation, we first performed a number of preliminary sensitivity tests. Values of the net employment effect were computed for a given set of base parameter values and DFI vector; next, the parameters in each of the industrial sectors were varied sequentially by 1% and the resulting percentage effect on net employment in each sector was obtained. From these "elasticities" it was possible to identify sectors in which precise estimates of σ, χ, and γ are crucial to the calculation.

These sensitivity tests were done for a number of different combinations of base values and DFI inputs. A sample of the results using 1970 DFI figures, σ equal to 1.0 and both χ and γ equal to zero, is shown in Table 2 of Appendix C. In general, the effects of variations or errors in χ and γ are small.

Variations in σ, however, have a stronger effect on total job loss—particularly in sectors (9) Machinery and (11) Transportation—not only because of the substantial volume of DFI in these sectors in the 1970 sample, but also because of larger intermediate requirements in those industries. Also the rather weak sensitivity of the overall calculation to changes in σ for sector (3) Petroleum is worth noting. This is due to both a relatively low labor–capital ratio and to small intermediate good requirements in that industry.

Because of the general sensitivity of our final results to the value of σ, our calculations of the net employment impact were carried out in several versions. In Table 3 we show the net employment impact for 1970 DFI using our best estimates of σ, obtained in Chapter III above. In Table 4, we also show the net employment effect over a range of alternative assumed values for σ from 0.1 to 1.0. (In these calculations χ equals its 1970 historical value and γ equals zero.

TABLE 3

Employment Effect of 1970 Vector[a]

Industry number	Industry name	DFI ($1000)	Total Employment impact (no. of jobs lost)	Demand displacement effect (no. of jobs lost)	Export stimulus effect (no. of jobs gained)	Employment impact (direct), first-round only (no. of jobs lost)
1	Agriculture, forestry, and fisheries	71,331	4751	13,522	8771	1273
2	Mining	884,885	189	1750	1561	0
3	Petroleum	2,721,572	702	1637	935	0
4	Food products	266,879	6835	8371	1536	6093
5	Paper and allied products	320,929	7231	9357	2126	4655
6	Chemicals and allied products	882,445	14,944	18,194	3250	10,646
7	Rubber and miscellaneous plastic products (finished)	123,594	5062	7731	2669	3731
8	Primary and fabricated metals	336,535	8854	27,826	18,972	3413
9	Machinery (except electrical)	1,242,846	46,905	54,499	10,594	40,749
10	Electrical machinery, equipment and supplies	359,044	17,620	25,202	7582	14,434

11	Transportation equipment	782,366	7210	15,039	7830	10,463
12	Other manufacturing	365,534	4439	14,585	10,146	403
13	Transportation, communication, and public utilities	399,617	1033	12,450	8417	0
14	Trade	701,797	8374	25,293	16,918	0
15	Banking and insurance, and miscellaneous industries	532,355	25,310	42,958	17,649	16,321
16	Post Office, Commodity Credit Corporation, and other federal enterprises	0	575	1948	1374	0
17	State and local government enterprises	0	344	1137	794	0
18	Directly allocated imports	0	0	0	0	0
19	Transferred imports	0	0	0	0	0
20	Business travel, entertainment, and gifts	0	0	0	0	0
21	Office supplies	0	0	0	0	0
	Total	9,991,729	160,377	281,500	121,123	112,182

[a] Here σ_i = value in column (4), Table 1, Chapter III; χ_i = historical value; $\gamma_i = 0.0$.

TABLE 4

1970 Employment effect of DFI for various assumed values of σ^a

Industry number	Industry name	DFI ($1000)	Total employment impact (no. of jobs lost)						
			$\sigma = 0.1$	$\sigma = 0.2$	$\sigma = 0.3$	$\sigma = 0.4$	$\sigma = 0.6$	$\sigma = 0.8$	$\sigma = 1.0$
1	Agriculture, forestry and, fisheries	71,331	−4931	−1091	2750	6590	14,270	21,951	29,631
2	Mining	884,885	1681	4923	8165	11,407	17,892	24,376	30,860
3	Petroleum	2,721,572	1522	3979	6436	8893	13,807	18,721	23,635
4	Food products	266,879	854	3243	5633	8023	12,802	17,582	22,361
5	Paper and allied products	320,929	260	2647	5034	7420	12,193	16,967	21,740
6	Chemicals and allied products	882,445	1333	5917	10,500	15,083	24,250	33,417	42,583
7	Rubber and miscellaneous plastic products (finished)	123,594	−569	1531	3630	5730	9930	14,129	18,329
8	Primary and fabricated metals	336,535	−8986	1000	10,986	20,972	40,945	60,917	80,889
9	Machinery (except electrical)	1,242,846	5724	22,041	38,358	54,676	87,310	119,945	152,580
10	Electrical machinery, equipment and supplies	359,044	318	8218	16,118	24,018	39,817	55,617	71,417

11	Transportation equipment	782,366	181	8192	16,203	24,214	40,236	56,257	72,279
12	Other manufacturing	365,534	−5080	−15	5051	10,116	20,247	30,378	40,509
13	Transportation, communication, and public utilities	399,617	−3083	2252	7587	12,922	23,591	34,261	44,930
14	Trade	701,797	3289	23,497	43,705	63,912	104,328	144,743	185,159
15	Banking and insurance, and miscellaneous industries	532,355	−2955	11,739	26,432	41,126	70,513	99,900	129,287
16	Post Office, Commodity Credit Corporation and other federal enterprises	0	−563	248	1058	1869	3490	5111	6732
17	State and local government enterprises	0	−305	183	672	1160	2137	3113	4090
18	Directly allocated imports	0	0	0	0	0	0	0	0
19	Transferred imports	0	0	0	0	0	0	0	0
20	Business travel, entertainment, and gifts	0	0	0	0	0	0	0	0
21	Office supplies	0	0	0	0	0	0	0	0
	Total	9,991,729	−11,310	98,504	208,317	318,131	290,472	757,384	977,011

[a] χ_i = historical values, $\gamma_i = 0$.

The employment effects for other years' DFI vectors are shown in Appendix C, Table 3.) The results of these estimations tend to underscore our earlier remarks about the sensitivity of the calculation to values of σ. For example, using our best estimates of σ, the net employment effect of DFI is an annual job loss of between 120,000 and 160,000 jobs. This job loss, however, is distributed rather unevenly over the various industrial sectors. Among the manufacturing sectors (for the 1970 DFI vector) the job loss is strongest in (9) Machinery, (10) Electrical Machinery, and (6) Chemicals; on the other hand the job loss in sectors where the value of σ is small or zero, such as (3) Petroleum, (4) Mining, (14) Trade, and (13) Transportation is small. Also, as σ is increased from 0.1 to 1.0, the net employment effect goes from a *net gain* of 11,000 jobs to a *net loss* of nearly one million jobs.

This variance suggests that it may be extremely useful to establish a "break-even" value of σ to use as a benchmark. This break-even σ level is defined as the level of σ at which the export displacement effect expressed in equation (1) is exactly offset by the export stimulus effect shown in equation (2). At the break-even level of σ the net employment impact of the given DFI vector is zero. This break-even value can be compared to any assumed or estimated value of σ to gauge whether the net job impact of DFI is positive or negative.

Algebraically, the break-even sigma, $\bar{\sigma}$, is expressed by

$$\bar{\sigma} = \frac{[1]'[l][[I - A]^{-1}[\chi] - [\chi]][q][\Delta F]}{[1]'[[l][q][\Delta F] + [l][[I - A]^{-1} - [I]][q][\Delta F]]}. \tag{5}$$

Using historical values of χ, γ equal to zero, and the 1970 DFI vector, the value of $\bar{\sigma}$ turns out to be approximately 0.11. Since the values for σ in manufacturing industries that we estimated earlier are well above these levels, one conclusion is quite evident. This calculation strongly suggests that the employment effect of DFI is a net job loss. The size of that loss, however, is much less certain.

The reader should be reminded that these conclusions assume that the substitution effects measured by σ are short-run in nature. As was pointed out earlier, it is quite possible that as new competitors to the MNC enter its market, the elasticity facing the firm increases and the measured value of σ may decline. In fact, if either the cost advantage of foreign production is sufficiently large or the market is highly competitive, home firms may reach their shutdown point and σ will become effectively zero. The latter possibility is not taken into account in our calculations because of data deficiency. On the other hand, for a similar reason our estimates of the true value of σ for new investment may have been somewhat underestimated. This is due to the fact that products associated with new DFI are quite likely to have a lower demand elasticity and, therefore, a higher value of σ than that of the entire output from cumulative past DFI. On the basis of the information available now, however, it is impossible to make any assessment of the size of these possible influences.

By this point it should be apparent from the considerable number of qualifications that have been made that the findings from the above exercises are tentative indeed. We stress that they should be regarded primarily as illustrative of basic techniques and suggestive of no more than the scale and direction of main effects—certainly not the final word on estimates of specific values. The general approach developed here is rich enough that a number of extensions immediately suggest themselves. An application to the skill composition of unemployment is illustrated in the next chapter. However, before these and related findings can become a sure basis for informed judgments on policy questions a thorough refining of basic data inputs is needed. Quite aside from the difficulties encountered in estimating σ, χ, and γ that were discussed previously, there are a number of other fundamental problems involved in the data handling that require considerable attention before any major extensions are attempted. In this regard, the formation of capital–output ratios, the deflation of DFI data to common-year, constant-dollar values, the blow-up of sample data to universe estimates, the use of 1970 I–O coefficients for all calculations, and even the determination of a common industry classification scheme all were of necessity somewhat inexact. Seen in this light, the shortcomings of the model developed in the chapters above should suggest an agenda for future data collection in this area.

Chapter VI

The Effect of DFI on the Occupational Composition of Domestic Employment Demand

During the postwar period, the American economy has experienced increasing difficulty in achieving full employment with price stability. Economists believe that one major source of this difficulty has been an imbalance in the composition of the demand for labor. As the economy moves through an expansion phase, shortages are observed to occur in certain labor force groups long before other groups even come close to attaining full employment. Skilled workers, for example, are frequently seen to have very low rates of unemployment and rapid rates of wage advance at the same time that less skilled workers are experiencing high unemployment rates and wage stagnation.

In a market economy in which resources are freely mobile, a natural response to a situation of this type is for employers to seek means of circumventing the labor market bottlenecks. In the case of multinationals, this could be done either by switching to domestic production processes that are more intensive in the use of less scarce groups, or by relocating production operations overseas. The former strategy will in every case alleviate the problem of domestic labor market bottlenecks, but may not be feasible if technical substitution possibilities are limited. When production is transferred overseas, the effect on labor market bottlenecks is less clear. If the production processes that are transferred abroad are relatively intensive in the use of the most scarce categories of skilled labor, these transfers will reduce the problem of bottlenecks. Indeed, one might expect that pressures to transfer processes of this type would be greatest, and that foreign investment might therefore tend to improve the composition of domestic labor demands. If the activities that are transferred abroad are intensive in their use of the relatively abundant labor categories, however, foreign investment will tend to exacerbate the bottlenecks problem. In these cases the fiscal or monetary stimulus that moves to combat the unemployment associated with the overseas transfer of production will leave the composition of demand even more heavily weighted in favor of scarce skill categories than before.

In order to determine whether foreign investment improves or worsens the problem of bottlenecks in the labor market, it is necessary first to establish a criterion by which to measure imbalances in the composition of demand for labor. The theoretical concept that underlies this criterion is the model of unemployment dispersion and wage inflation introduced by Lipsey.[1] Lipsey's model considers a group of identical labor submarkets and concludes that wage-inflation pressures are minimized for a given aggregate unemployment rate when the unemployment rates in all the submarkets are equal. Lipsey's model has been generalized for the case of submarkets which have different wage levels,[2] a more realistic description of submarkets defined by skill category. Here the conclusion is that the least inflationary distribution of demands calls for relatively high unemployment rates in those submarkets with relatively high wage rates and vice versa.[3] In terms of skill

---

[1] See Lipsey (1960).

[2] See Cook and Frank (1975).

[3] With two submarkets the inflation minimizing distribution of employment rates must satisfy

$$\frac{e_1}{e_2} = \frac{w_2 g_2'(e_2)}{w_1 g_1'(e_1)},$$

where w_i is the wage rate, e_i the employment rate and $g_i'(e_i)$ the slope of the Phillips curve for the ith market. See Cook and Frank (1975, p. 244).

categories, a balanced composition of demand is one in which more skilled (high-wage) groups have high unemployment rates while less skilled (low-wage) groups have low unemployment rates.[4] Since the present distribution of unemployment across skill categories is precisely the reverse of the optimal distribution—more skilled groups now have the lowest unemployment rates—the generalized dispersion model reinforces a basic conclusion of the Lipsey model: any shift in the composition of demand in the direction of greater equality across skill categories constitutes a clear improvement over the composition of demand currently observed in the United States.

Employing this criterion, we have attempted to answer the question of whether DFI improves or makes worse the problem of structural imbalances in the occupational distribution of employment demand. To do this we have employed data from the 1970 *National Industry Occupational Employment Matrix* (U.S. Bureau of Labor Statistics, 1971) in conjunction with our estimates of industry substitution ratios in carrying out an input–output calculation of the type described in the previous chapter.[5] The results of this calculation for the 1970 flow of DFI are reproduced in Table 1 below for a four-order breakdown of occupational categories.

Column 1 of Table 1 lists the estimated employment demand reductions by occupational category. Column 2 lists total 1970 employment in these categories. In column 3 we have shown employment demand reduction ratios by occupational category, calculated as 100 times the ratio of occupational employment demand reduction to total occupational employment. Column 4 shows the 1970 occupational unemployment rates.

Most of the employment demand reductions are concentrated on white and blue-collar workers, with service and farm workers experiencing only comparatively minor effects. Among the former

---

[4] The submarkets with the higher wage rate must have a higher unemployment rate if wage inflation is to be minimized because of the larger than proportional contribution of the high-wage submarket to the overall wage index. A given increase in unemployment is worth just as much in the low-wage submarket as it would be in the high-wage submarket, but produces a smaller boost in the aggregate rate of wage inflation when taken in the low-wage submarket.

[5] The short-run impact study produced a vector of job loss effects by industry, $[\Delta L_i]$. To find the effect of this job loss by skill categories, this vector was pre-multiplied by a matrix, $[S_{ij}]$, where each entry measured the percentage of 1970 employment in industry i in skill class j.

TABLE 1

*Employment demand reductions from 1970 DFI vector
by occupational category (4-order)*

Occupational category	(1) Employment demand reduction (thousands)	(2) Employment (thousands)	(3) Demand reduction ratio $(1) \div (2) \times 100$	(4) 1970 unemployment rate (%)
White collar	62.2	37,997	0.164	2.8
Blue collar	85.4	27,791	0.307	6.2
Service	8.6	9712	0.088	5.3
Farm workers	4.2	3124	0.134	2.6

categories, blue-collar workers are by far the hardest hit. In terms of our criterion for a balanced composition of demand, the entries of Table 1 suggest strongly that the foreign investment flows of 1970 have exacerbated the problem of structural bottlenecks in the labor market.[6] "Blue-collar" and "white-collar" are extremely aggregative occupational categories, and our conclusions might be modified somewhat if employment demand reductions were concentrated on high-wage groups within each category. In order to investigate this possibility, we have repeated the original calculations on the basis of a 9-order occupational breakdown. These results appear in Table 2. Within the white-collar category, employment demand reductions are not highly concentrated within any of the four subgroups shown in Table 2. Accordingly, we conclude that the entries in Table 2 are generally consistent with the hypothesis that foreign investment outflows tend to create additional imbalances in the composition of demand for labor.

At this point we should stress that, for a number of reasons, the estimates reported in Table 1 and 2 should be regarded as tentative in character. Because we lacked specific information on the types of activities that are transferred abroad, we constructed Tables 1 and 2 under the assumption that the labor requirements associated with each unit of export stimulus and export displacement are the same as the overall labor requirements vector for the particular industry in which

---

[6] A very similar pattern of results emerged when the same calculations were carried out for the remaining years in the 1966–1973 period for which we have data.

TABLE 2

Employment demand reductions from 1970 DFI vector by occupational category (9-order)

Occupational category (technical and kindred)	(1) Employment demand reduction (thousands)	(2) Employment (thousands)	(3) Demand reduction ratio, (1) ÷ (2) × 100	(4) 1970 unemployment rate (%)
White collar				
Professional,	21.7	11,140	0.195	2.0
Managers, officials, and proprietors	11.9	8289	0.141	1.3
Clerical and kindred	23.5	13,714	0.171	4.0
Sales workers	5.2	4854	0.106	3.9
Blue collar				
Craftsmen, foremen and kindred	29.4	10,158	0.289	3.8
Operatives	49.7	13,909	0.357	7.1
Laborers, except farm and mines	6.3	3724	0.169	9.5
Service workers	8.6	9712	0.088	5.3
Farmers and farm workers	4.2	3124	0.133	2.6
Totals	160.3	78,627	0.203	4.9

69

they occur. Some other researchers who have addressed the issue of the effect of DFI on the composition of demand for labor have argued that multinationals tend to export production activities to overseas sites while concentrating management and other front office support activities in domestic sites.[7] If so, our estimates in Tables 1 and 2 will tend to understate the increase in structural imbalances in the labor market that result from capital outflows. On the other hand, there is some indication that the firms most heavily involved in foreign investment activities may employ production processes that are more technology-intensive than those employed by other firms. If so, and if such technologies are relatively intensive in their requirements for skilled labor categories, our estimates will tend to overstate the occupational labor demand imbalance associated with DFI.

Finally, all of the occupational employment demand reduction estimates are based on our earlier estimates of the home–foreign substitution ratios and accordingly are subject to the same qualifications that apply to these.

With these qualifications in mind, our estimates of the occupational employment demand effects of DFI provide no support for the hypothesis that the desire to escape domestic labor market bottlenecks is the primary motive for the establishment of foreign subsidiaries by MNCs. On the contrary, our estimates seem to suggest that foreign investment is, if anything, a cause rather than an effect of domestic labor market bottlenecks.[8] To be sure, DFI is not the only cause of such bottlenecks and the magnitudes of the effects we estimate are small enough to suggest that the problem of poorly distributed demands in the labor market would be with us for quite some time even if new foreign investments were prohibited altogether.

---

[7] See, for example, Hawkins (1972b) and U.S. Tariff Commission (1973).

[8] This interpretation is consistent with the widely held belief that multinationals go abroad primarily because of the multiple cost advantages of locating production facilities in close proximity with the markets they serve.

Chapter VII

Short-Run Labor Market Adjustments to Unemployment Resulting from Overseas Production Transfers

In this chapter we employ a simple probabilistic model of the labor market in an attempt to simulate the time profile of industry unemployment as it responds to an initial DFI-related displacement of workers.

Previous discussions of the effect of DFI on unemployment have produced estimates of the total number of jobs lost by cumulating the equivalent of our employment demand reduction estimates over a rather long historical period. The U.S. Tariff Commission, for example, has estimated that as many as 1.3 million jobs may have been lost because of the stock of foreign investments in place as of 1970 (U.S. Tariff Commission, 1973). Estimates such as these shed very little light on the question of how much of our current domestic unemployment is the result of DFI. Most workers who lost their jobs when plants moved abroad during the mid-sixties have presumably either retired, died, or found new jobs in the meantime. Accordingly, explicit account of labor market adjustment processes must be taken in order to generate even a crude picture of the actual unemployment that results from overseas investment.

Contemporary discussions of the problem of unemployment have stressed its dynamic character. The flows into and out of unemployment are very substantial in relation to the stock of unemployed individuals and spells of unemployment are of short average duration. A certain degree of job turnover is inherent in the normal functioning of any labor market, and even under equilibrium conditions one observes simultaneously a group of unemployed job seekers and a collection of unfilled job vacancies. Under given institutional conditions, the likelihood that a job seeker will be placed in a job during a certain time period will depend on the overall balance between these vacancies and searchers. In an expanding sector, for example, in which vacancies greatly outnumber searchers, the likelihood of a rapid placement is high in comparison with that of a contracting sector.

In our exercise, we consider a situation in which each industry labor market is in an initial state of equilibrium in which vacancies and searchers are approximately in balance. The first impact of overseas production transfers for a given industry is taken to be the addition to the unemployed pool of a group of workers whose number is determined by the size of the export displacement effect for that industry as calculated in Chapter V. Simultaneously, the industry adds a number of vacancies determined in accordance with the size of the export stimulus effect, also as calculated in Chapter V. Because the export displacement effect outweighs the export stimulus effect for every industry in our study, the outcome of these additions is to increase the ratio of unemployed job seekers to unfilled vacancies. This, in turn, reduces an individual searcher's probability per period of successful job placement. We employ this reduced placement probability to estimate the number of searchers who will find jobs during the next period.

The normal turnover process is presumed all the while to generate flows of new searchers and vacancies each period. These flows are used in conjunction with the estimated placement outcomes from the previous period to determine a new placement probability for the next period. The same calculations are then performed for successive periods until most of the originally displaced workers have secured new jobs. Once most of these placements have occurred, the labor market will have moved to a state in which the flows into and out of unemployment are again equal. Even though the flow balance is restored, the stock of job seekers will continue to be larger than the stock of vacancies until aggregate policies can act to restore demand.[1] As a result, the probability per period of successful job placement will be less than it was originally, even after all of the workers displaced by the production transfer have found new jobs.

Our model thus points to two types of unemployment that are attributable to overseas production transfers. The first and most visible of these is the joblessness experienced by those workers directly displaced by the production transfers. The second and somewhat more subtle type results from the fact that the employment demand reductions reduce placement probabilities for all job seekers, so that even those not displaced directly by the production transfer will take longer on average to secure new jobs.

Using methods and data that are described in detail in Appendix D, we have estimated adjustment profiles for the initially displaced workers in eight large manufacturing industries. These estimates are reported in Tables 1 and 2. Row 1 of Table 1 records the number of layoffs (in thousands) associated with the 1970 export displacement effect for each industry. Successive rows of Table 1 list our estimates of the number of these initially displaced workers who remain unemployed on successive weeks from the layoff date. Table 2 translates the entries of Table 1 into proportional terms; its ith row entries are interpreted as the fractions of the originally displaced cohorts that remain unemployed i weeks from the layoff date.

The most striking feature of the estimates reported in Tables 1 and 2 is that, for most industries, a majority of the displaced workers will have found new jobs within five weeks of the date of the onset of their unemployment. The nonelectrical machinery industry, which experiences the largest initial job displacement, also exhibits the most seriously persistent unemployment problem, but even in this case more than 75% of the initially displaced workers will have found new jobs within 16 weeks of their layoff dates. While we feel that every

---

[1] Or until a fall in wages can accomplish the same result.

TABLE 1

Direct unemployment resulting from 1970 DFI vector: initially displaced workers who remain unemployed (thousands)

Weeks from layoff date	Industry								
	Food	Paper	Chemicals	Rubber	Metals	Nonelectrical machinery	Electrical machinery	Transportation equipment
0	8.371	9.357	18.194	7.731	27.826	54.500	25.202	15.039
1	7.050	8.202	16.068	6.757	23.951	49.333	22.660	13.387
2	5.967	7.212	14.230	5.924	20.694	44.756	20.412	11.943
3	5.073	6.359	12.634	5.209	17.944	40.686	18.421	10.676
4	4.332	5.621	11.245	4.593	15.612	37.056	16.652	9.563
5	3.716	4.982	10.032	4.060	13.628	33.808	15.079	8.582
6	3.198	4.426	8.969	3.599	11.932	30.895	13.676	7.716
7	2.763	3.941	8.035	3.197	10.478	28.276	12.423	6.950
8	2.396	3.517	7.213	2.847	9.226	25.916	11.301	6.271
9	2.084	3.146	6.487	2.541	8.146	23.784	10.296	5.668

74

10	1.819	2.819	5.845	2.272	7.210	21.856	9.393	5.131
11	1.592	2.531	5.276	2.036	6.398	20.109	8.580	4.653
12	1.398	2.277	4.770	1.828	5.690	18.523	7.849	4.225
13	1.231	2.052	4.328	1.644	5.072	17.081	7.188	3.842
14	1.086	1.852	3.918	1.482	4.531	15.768	6.592	3.500
15	0.961	1.675	3.559	1.338	4.056	14.571	6.052	3.192
16	0.853	1.517	3.238	1.210	3.638	13.478	5.563	2.915
17	0.758	1.376	2.950	1.096	3.269	12.480	5.119	2.665
18	0.676	1.250	2.691	0.994	2.943	11.566	4.715	2.440
19	0.603	1.137	2.458	0.903	2.654	10.729	4.348	2.237
20	0.540	1.036	2.249	0.821	2.398	9.962	4.014	2.053
21	0.484	0.946	2.060	0.748	2.170	9.257	3.709	1.887
22	0.435	0.864	1.889	0.683	1.966	8.610	3.431	1.736
23	0.391	0.790	1.734	0.624	1.785	8.014	3.177	1.598
24	0.353	0.724	1.594	0.571	1.623	7.466	2.944	1.473
25	0.318	0.664	1.466	0.523	1.477	6.961	2.731	1.360
26	0.288	0.609	1.351	0.479	1.347	6.495	2.535	1.256
52	0.034	0.097	0.229	0.075	0.188	1.412	0.500	0.225

SOURCE: See Appendix D.

TABLE 2

Direct unemployment resulting from 1970 DFI vector:
fraction of initially displaced workers who remain unemployed

Weeks from layoff date	Industry							
	Food	Paper	Chemicals	Rubber	Metals	Nonelectrical machinery	Electrical machinery	Transportation equipment
0	1.000	1.000	1.000	1.000	1.000	1.000	1.000	1.000
1	0.842	0.877	0.883	0.874	0.861	0.905	0.899	0.890
2	0.713	0.771	0.782	0.766	0.744	0.821	0.810	0.794
3	0.606	0.680	0.694	0.674	0.645	0.747	0.731	0.710
4	0.518	0.601	0.618	0.594	0.561	0.680	0.661	0.636
5	0.444	0.532	0.551	0.525	0.490	0.620	0.598	0.571
6	0.382	0.473	0.493	0.465	0.429	0.567	0.543	0.513
7	0.330	0.421	0.442	0.414	0.377	0.519	0.493	0.462
8	0.286	0.376	0.396	0.368	0.332	0.476	0.448	0.417
9	0.249	0.336	0.357	0.329	0.293	0.436	0.409	0.377
10	0.217	0.301	0.321	0.294	0.259	0.401	0.373	0.341

11	0.190	0.278	0.290	0.263	0.230	0.369	0.349	0.309
12	0.167	0.243	0.262	0.236	0.204	0.340	0.311	0.281
13	0.147	0.219	0.237	0.213	0.182	0.313	0.285	0.256
14	0.130	0.198	0.215	0.192	0.163	0.289	0.262	0.233
15	0.115	0.175	0.196	0.173	0.146	0.267	0.240	0.212
16	0.102	0.162	0.178	0.156	0.131	0.247	0.221	0.194
17	0.091	0.147	0.162	0.142	0.117	0.229	0.203	0.177
18	0.081	0.134	0.148	0.128	0.106	0.212	0.187	0.162
19	0.072	0.122	0.135	0.117	0.095	0.197	0.173	0.149
20	0.064	0.111	0.124	0.106	0.086	0.183	0.159	0.137
21	0.058	0.101	0.113	0.097	0.078	0.170	0.147	0.125
22	0.052	0.092	0.104	0.088	0.071	0.158	0.136	0.115
23	0.047	0.084	0.095	0.081	0.064	0.147	0.126	0.106
24	0.042	0.077	0.089	0.074	0.058	0.137	0.117	0.098
25	0.038	0.070	0.081	0.068	0.053	0.128	0.106	0.090
26	0.034	0.065	0.074	0.062	0.048	0.119	0.101	0.084
52	0.004	0.010	0.013	0.010	0.007	0.026	0.020	0.015

SOURCE: See Appendix D.

policy effort should be made to expedite job placement and provide interim income maintenance for workers whose jobs are lost for whatever reason, we conclude from the unemployment profiles in Tables 1 and 2 that protracted periods of joblessness are not one of the major welfare costs associated with the overseas transfer of production activities.

In Table 3 we summarize our estimates of the indirect unemployment that results from DFI. Columns 1–4 of Table 3 report weekly job placement probabilities by industry and the corresponding average unemployment durations both before the 1970 DFI displacement occurs and again after the initially displaced workers have found new jobs. Column 5 reports "residual unemployment" by industry, which is the increase in the stock of unemployed workers associated with the higher average durations of unemployment that result from the reduced labor demands that attend overseas production transfers.

The numbers in Tables 1–3 are displayed graphically in Figs. 1–8. In these diagrams, cumulative percentages are displayed at five-week intervals to indicate the fraction of workers initially displaced who have successfully secured new jobs. As it was in the case of direct unemployment effects, the nonelectrical machinery industry is hardest hit with respect to indirect effects. Its average duration of unemployment rises by nearly four weeks because of the employment demand reductions stemming from 1970 DFI. Even after those workers directly displaced by DFI have found new jobs, this higher duration of unemployment results in an increase of almost 42,000 in the nonelectrical machinery industry's stock of unemployed job seekers. The indirect effects are markedly smaller in all the other industries but are nonetheless

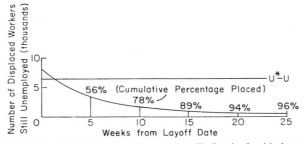

FIGURE 1   1970 DFI unemployment profile for the food industry.

TABLE 3

Indirect unemployment resulting from 1970 DFI

Industry	Average weekly placement probability		Average duration of unemployment (weeks)		Number unemployed		Residual unemployed, $U^* - U_0$
	Pre-1970 DFI, $\bar{p}_{s0}$	Post-1970 DFI, $\bar{p}_s^*$	Pre-1970 DFI, $\bar{d}_{s0}$	Post-1970 DFI, $\bar{d}_s^*$	Pre-1970 DFI, U_0	Post-1970 DFI, U^*	
Food	0.142	0.134	6.99	7.38	120,749	127,153	6404
Paper	0.123	0.104	8.05	9.46	40,528	47,369	6841
Chemicals	0.123	0.098	8.05	10.00	60,325	74,462	14,137
Rubber	0.123	0.106	8.05	9.28	32,599	37,388	4789
Metals	0.125	0.118	7.90	8.40	138,725	147,145	8420
Nonelectrical machinery	0.116	0.077	8.53	12.49	90,398	132,372	41,974
Electrical machinery	0.098	0.085	10.03	11.45	117,810	134,408	16,598
Transportation equipment	0.098	0.093	10.03	10.51	143,622	150,305	6683

SOURCE: See Apppendix D.

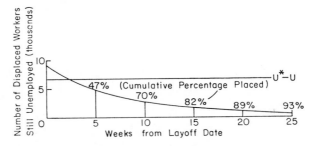

FIGURE 2   1970 DFI unemployment profile for the paper industry.

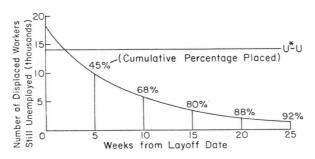

FIGURE 3   1970 DFI unemployment profile for the chemicals industry.

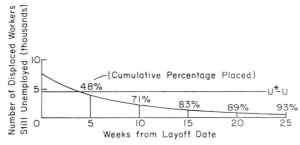

FIGURE 4   1970 DFI unemployment profile for the rubber industry.

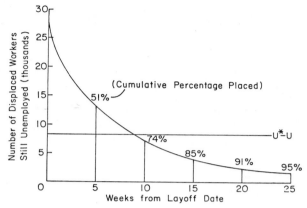

FIGURE 5   1970 DFI unemployment profile for the metals industry.

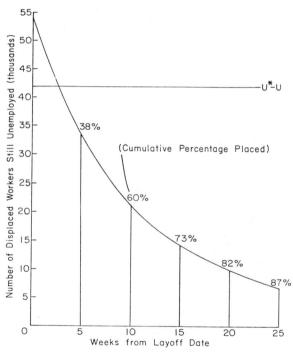

FIGURE 6   1970 DFI unemployment profile for the nonelectrical machinery industry.

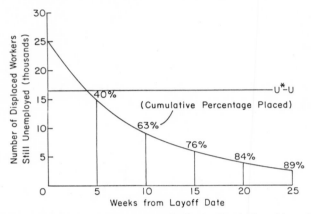

FIGURE 7   1970 DFI unemployment profile for the electrical machinery industry.

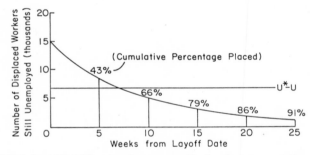

FIGURE 8   1970 DFI unemployment profile for the transportation equipment industry.

substantial in several, especially electrical machinery and chemicals. As illustrated in Figs. 1–8, the residual unemployment increases constitute a large share of the initial displacements in every industry.

At the micro level, these residual unemployment increases constitute a smaller social burden than might at first appear, inasmuch as they are the result of an increase in the average duration of a spell of unemployment of less than two weeks. On the other hand, when viewed in terms of their implied costs in output forgone, the residual unemployment figures appear much more significant.

Like the direct unemployment effects, the residual effects are a transitory phenomenon; they will tend to decay as real wages adjust and as the employment demand reductions from which they stem are made the subject of attack by aggregate demand policy. How long these effects will take to disappear, however, remains an open question.

In Appendix D we discuss a number of qualifications that should be borne in mind when interpreting the findings reported in Tables 1–3. The general flavor of these qualifications is that the estimates of the size of the initial displacements are rather more uncertain than are those of the indirect effects. We also stress that any inferences that may be drawn from our calculations in this section will in general be pertinent only to labor markets whose degree of tightness is roughly the same as that of the 1970 labor market. Particular care should be taken to avoid any inference that our estimates are indicative of what the time profiles of DFI-related unemployment would be like in, say, the 1978 labor market with its much higher unemployment rate.

Chapter VIII

The Long-Run Distributional
Consequences of Overseas Investment

Up to this point our study has been primarily short run in focus, and analysis of the domestic labor market dislocations associated with direct foreign investment has been constructed from essentially microeconomic considerations of firm, industry, and labor market behavior. While this emphasis is appropriate for the short run, analysis of related long-run issues should be based on a wider view. Inasmuch as the aggregate economy can adjust eventually to DFI-related dislocations through either market forces or direct policy intervention, in a long-run context our attention must shift to such issues as the effect of DFI on the equilibrium level and distribution of U.S. income.

Is it the case, for example, as some proponents of foreign investment have suggested, that DFI raises the levels of both U.S. corporate and wage incomes from what they would otherwise be? Or, at the other extreme, can DFI actually reduce not only the level of wage income, but even the overall level of national income available to the U.S. economy?

85

Answering questions of this nature clearly demands a much broader approach. Issues which could safely be disregarded in earlier sections — such as the effects of DFI on capital markets, on the foreign exchange market, and on aggregate investment and savings—now become relevant. Tracing out these interactions and still retaining the degree of industry and market detail of previous sections, however, would be an unmanagable task. Accordingly, in this section we shall shift to the other end of the analytical spectrum and consider the effects of DFI on the domestic economy within a dynamic, general equilibrium framework. In taking this approach we shall forego much of the detail of earlier sections. However, by preserving the essential characteristics of an aggregate program of direct foreign investment, we can illustrate the main features of its long-run interaction with the domestic economy.

To many observers the foreign investment boom of the 1960s and early 1970s was based primarily on what may be described broadly as gaps in technology. In this view, U.S. firms with access to superior technical information, unique products, better organizational and managerial skills, or some other appropriable advantage invested in overseas operations to realize the full return on their implicit market power. The key factor in the foreign investment process was the package of technical and entrepreneurial skills that accompanied the international movement of capital. Indeed, foreign investment has been regarded as one of the main vehicles for international transfer of technology in this broad sense.[1] Accordingly, for purposes of aggregate analysis, it will be convenient to regard DFI as a combination of capital flow and technology transfer.

Analysis of foreign investment issues is made slightly more complicated by recent changes in the international environment in which multinationals operate and by changes in corporate strategy. For a

---

[1] The role of foreign investment as a device for technology transfer is discussed in greater detail in Kindleberger (1969), Caves (1971), and Musgrave (1975). This aspect deserves special emphasis here inasmuch as it has largely been ignored in macroeconomic, general equilibrium treatments of foreign investment. In fact, it has been frequently argued that the very basis for most recent U.S. foreign investment in manufacturing is the transfer to overseas locations of just such special advantages. A similar view of foreign investment is imbedded in the so-called "product cycle" theories developed by Vernon (1966) and others. A general theory of foreign investment along these lines is developed in Magee (1977).

number of reasons, the previously rapid pace of foreign investment expansion has slackened since the early 1970s. At the same time, it appears that a growing number of U.S. firms are shifting to a strategy of direct transfer of proprietary technology without risking financial capital—primarily through licensing arrangements with foreign affiliates.[2] In many instances, the technology being sold is of the most recent generation, in contrast to earlier direct transfers which usually involved more mature products and a more generally available type of information. To the extent that this represents a widespread phenomenon, licensing raises issues similar to those raised by DFI. What are the implications of such a program of direct technology transfer without capital flow for the equilibrium level of U.S. income? How are domestic income levels and shares likely to be affected by a widespread shift away from indirect technology transfer through foreign investment and toward direct transfer through licensing?

In order to consider these and similar questions this chapter is organized in the following way. First, we develop a general equilibrium model in which foreign investment is treated as a capital flow with technology transfer. This model is then used to estimate the effects of foreign investment on principal economic aggregates. Next, this basic model is subjected to two major modifications. In the first of these, we explore the feedback to savings from changes in the distribution of domestic income induced by direct foreign investment. In a later section, the model is modified to describe the effects of international technology transfer without associated capital flow, i.e., the case of pure licensing.

Before turning to the models and their implications the reader should be forewarned of the limitations of this type of analysis. First, inasmuch as the basic DFI model and licensing model embody polar assumptions about the degree of capital movement associated with technology transfer, neither gives a very exact representation of the actual state of the world. Although we would argue that the basic DFI model comes much closer to characterizing the situation in 1970 (the

---

[2] Some of the most important factors in this shift are uncertainty about exchange rates and overseas economic and political conditions, unanticipated capital shortages, higher costs of research and development, and increased technical capability in host countries. These developments and a number of case studies are discussed in Baranson (1976).

base year used for the empirical tests), the true state of the world almost surely lies somewhere between these extremes—both then and now.

Second, we should point out that a general equilibrium growth model is a very sensitive tool for empirical analysis. In large part, because of its high degree of aggregation, outcomes depend very closely on values assigned to a handful of key parameters and to assumptions about the structure of the model. Wherever possible we have taken care to base parameter values on best estimates. We have also carried out a series of sensitivity tests (discussed in Appendix E) to identify parameters for which variations or inaccurate measurement appear to affect the results most strongly. Finally, we have investigated how the model's performance and our main conclusions may be influenced by changes in its structure.

The general picture that emerges is one with a fairly wide range of outcomes. Accordingly, considerable care must be taken in interpreting the results. At most, these exercises provide some preliminary, qualitative answers to the questions that we have raised above. Our findings highlight the fact that a good deal of refinement of the basic data, of the model, and of the general technique itself is needed before quantitative estimates can be pinned down with precision.

Direct Foreign Investment in a Long-Run Model

In recent years foreign investment has been gradually integrated into single-period general equilibrium models, and the comparative statics of foreign investment in this type of framework has been explored quite thoroughly. For the most part, however, direct foreign investment has not been treated very extensively in dynamic models. From the point of view of analyzing the long-run effects of DFI, this is a potentially serious omission, since in some circumstances disregarding the dynamic linkages between foreign investment and the rest of the economy can give an inaccurate and misleading impression of the long-run consequences of a change in policy.

For example, as we have indicated earlier, one point of controversy in this area has been the question of the degree of substitution between home and foreign investment. Supporters of DFI have argued that only a very small part of U.S. overseas investment has occurred at the expense of comparable U.S. activity, and that if foreign investment were further restricted, the positive effect on domestic U.S. operations would be slight. Opponents, on the other hand, regard foreign investment as a direct substitute for its domestic counterpart. Although our attention in previous sections was focused on the short-run implications of home–foreign substitution, the question is of obvious significance in a long-run context as well, since a smaller domestic capital stock ordinarily implies lower wages and a decreased income share for labor.

The previous treatment of foreign investment in static neoclassical trade models has tended to reflect the direct substitution view.[3] In this approach, foreign investment is frequently regarded as the equivalent of a physical transfer of units of homogeneous capital inputs (within a fixed world stock) across international borders. Accordingly, the effective foreign capital stock is augmented by DFI and the domestic capital stock is reduced in a simple one-for-one fashion—just as if the corresponding physical machinery were unbolted and reinstalled abroad. In making such a conceptual simplification, however, this approach clearly predetermines the degree of home–foreign substitution.

In a more dynamic view, real foreign investment takes place as new capital goods are purchased by foreign subsidiaries from the output streams of both the host and home economies. The resulting changes in real capital stock in both locations will affect incomes, savings, capital formation, and local rates of return in subsequent periods—implying that additional rounds of capital movements and related adjustments must take place before the global economy is fully stabilized. Our notion of long-run equilibrium corresponds to the position of the economy after this full dynamic adjustment process has occurred. Although we shall spell out the conditions for long-run equilibrium more exactly in the formal model below, we point out here that when we measure the effects of foreign investment—including the degree of home–foreign substitution—we shall be comparing long-run equilibria of this type. As we shall see, when these dynamic effects are introduced, the degree of home–foreign substitution can vary over a rather wide range and is by no means restricted to a value of unity.

[3] See, for example, Kemp (1966), Jones (1967), and Chipman (1972).

The Foreign Investment Model

To analyze the long-run effects of foreign investment, we make use of the following relationships:

$$\theta(k - e) - \theta\psi e_F - e^*[1 - \theta(1 + \psi)] + (1 - \theta)k^* = 0, \qquad (1)$$

$$\theta\left[\frac{k(1 + \psi)}{e + (\psi e_F)} - 1\right] + (1 - \theta)\left[\frac{k^*}{e^*} - 1\right] = 0, \qquad (2)$$

$$f^*(e^*) - e^*f^{*\prime}(e^*) = f_F(e_F) - e_F f_F'(e_F), \qquad (3)$$

$$(1 - \tau)f'(e) = (1 - t)f_F'(e_F), \qquad (4)$$

$$\eta k = \zeta[f(e) + (1 - \tau^*)f_F'(e_F)(k - e)], \qquad (5)$$

where

k is the capital/labor ratio for factors *owned* by the home country,

k^* the capital/labor ratio for factors *owned* by the foreign country (assumed constant),

e the capital/labor ratio for factors *employed* in home production,

e_F the capital/labor ratio for factors *employed* in the foreign investment sector,

e^* the capital/labor ratio for factors *employed* in foreign production,

$f(e)$ the output per unit of labor in home production,

$f_F(e_F)$ the output per unit of labor in the foreign investment sector,

$f^*(e^*)$ the output per unit of labor in foreign production,

ψ the ratio of foreign labor employed in the foreign investment sector to labor employed at home,

θ the ratio of home labor to total world labor (constant),

η the growth rate of the home labor force plus the rate of capital stock depreciation (constant),

ζ the home average savings propensity (constant),

τ the home tax rate on domestic returns to capital (constant),

τ^* the foreign tax rate on foreign returns to capital (constant),

t the total tax rate (including both foreign and domestic taxes) on returns to foreign-invested capital (constant).

This model is basically an extension of the closed, single sector, neoclassical growth model to an open economy with foreign invest-ment.[4] One of its main innovations is the division of global production of the single undifferentiated product into three distinct activities, namely, production at home, production abroad by home entrepre-neurs (through foreign investment), and production abroad by foreign entrepreneurs. Although the basis for these distinctions is discussed more fully below, it should be noted here that each production sector is assigned its own factor employment ratio and production function. Since we assume that these production relationships exhibit constant returns to scale, the system is expressed in the convenient labor-intensive form.

Equations (1) and (2) are compact expressions of global full employment conditions. Taken together, they require that the total world stocks of capital and labor be fully utilized at all times by the three aggregate production sectors.[5] Equation (3) reflects the fact that foreign investors and local foreign producers share the same local market for foreign labor services. Since foreign labor is assumed to be undifferentiated, under perfectly competitive conditions wages are equalized across the two sectors, as indicated by equation (3). Equation (4) has a similar interpretation. U.S. investors are assumed to be willing to continue to relocate abroad until the after-tax return to foreign investment (i.e., the return after both foreign and U.S. taxes on cor-porate profits) equals the after-tax return to investment at home.[6]

Equations (1)–(4), which are assumed to hold in each period, in effect summarize the static properties of the system. Given a value for the domestic capital/labor ratio k, they allow us to determine the sec-toral distribution of factors and the level of factor returns. In this model, however, the long-run equilibrium level of k is endogenous to the system and is found by introducing equation (5). This equation expresses the key steady state condition that in long-run equilibrium

---

[4] For additional details on the properties of this class of model see, for example, Wan (1971). A somewhat similar model, without the technology refinements, appears in Frenkel (1971), Frenkel and Fischer (1972), and Neher (1970).

[5] Strictly speaking, equations (1) and (2) do not require full employment but only a constant degree of factor utilization.

[6] We have experimented with a version of this equation which allows for an untaxed depreciation allowance. Results are affected very little by this modification.

the investment required to offset depreciation of the domestically owned capital stock and growth in the labor force must exactly equal domestic savings. This condition is derived from the usual requirement that aggregate savings equal aggregate investment and from the fact that the dynamics of the system will tend to drive the capital/labor ratio k (and all other variables) to its long-run, steady state level.

This dynamic property can be understood better by referring to Fig. 1, which is a modified version of the phase diagram for a single-sector, closed economy. We let the function,

$$y = G(k) \equiv f(e) + [1 - \tau^*]f'_F(e_F)(k - e), \tag{6}$$

measure per capita national income, including the post–foreign tax (but pre–U.S. tax) earnings of foreign investment. Accordingly, the savings–investment equality for this economy can be written as

$$\zeta G(k) = \eta k + \dot{k}, \tag{7}$$

where $\dot{k}$ stands for the time rate of change of the capital/labor ratio k.

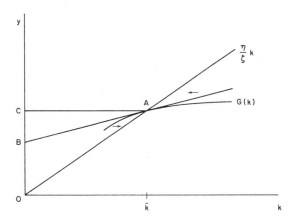

FIGURE 1 Modified phase diagram for a single-sector, closed economy. Because $\dot{k} = \zeta G(k) - \eta k$, and $G' < \eta/\zeta$, k will tend toward $\bar{k}$ and income toward the level shown at point A. The two construction lines, AB and AC, show how income is divided between savings and absorption of resources. AB has slope equal to η and AC is perpendicular to the vertical axis. Accordingly, BC measures steady state per capita savings and OB steady state per capita absorption.

If $G'(k) < \eta/\zeta$ for all values of k in the relevant range,[7] then this system will show the usual stability property, namely, that it will tend toward $\bar{k}$, the value of k for which $G(k) = \eta/\zeta$. At this value of k, $\dot{k}$ vanishes and equation (7) is identical to equation (5).

This property is shown by the position of the curves and the vectors indicating directions of motion in Fig. 1. When k exceeds $\bar{k}$, the steady state level, the investment necessary to maintain the domestic capital/labor ratio exceeds the level of savings generated. Hence, the capital/labor ratio falls, continuing to do so until k reaches $\bar{k}$. (A similar adjustment process applies on the low side of $\bar{k}$.) With each value of k are associated an allocation of factors to the three sectors and a set of factor returns. What we shall call the long-run equilibrium values of these are, of course, the ones associated with k and the values of the other four variables, e, e^*, e_F, and ψ, that simultaneously satisfy equations (1)–(4) and (5).

Although the equations above serve to identify the long-run global equilibrium, before we can estimate the effects of foreign investment we need to spell out the production relationships in greater detail. In this analysis, foreign investment is motivated by differences in production conditions across the three aggregate sectors. Although we assume that the three aggregate production functions are of similar general form, they are allowed to differ by scale parameters that reflect the influence of broadly defined "technology" differences. To be more specific, we distinguish two basic types. The first, which we shall designate as "labor-specific," refers to technological or cost differences associated with nonmobile factors of production. Systematic international differences in labor productivity provide an obvious illustration, but artificially low local wages, price distortions from domestic policy measures, or special access to local factors of production all can be regarded as having a similar effect on the aggregate production relation after making appropriate changes in the definition of its arguments. To capture these effects we shall assume that the home aggregate production function is related to that of the foreign investment sector as follows:

$$f(e) = \lambda f_F(e_F), \quad e = e_F, \tag{8}$$

[7] It can be shown that this condition is satisfied under not unduly restrictive assumptions on the structure and parameter values of the model.

where λ is a scale factor that reflects the influence of labor-specific differences. By this definition it should be clear that foreign investment is encouraged, *ceteris paribus*, by smaller values of λ.

Similarly, we also distinguish a second prototype case—the "capital-specific" case—in which access to special technological advantage is controlled by the internationally mobile factor (designated broadly as capital here). In this case technological advantages, whether embodied in patents, in industry-specific techniques, or simply in superior managerial expertise, can be utilized in the overseas site through foreign investment. It is, of course, this type of technology advantage, not the first, that is the basis for the technology transfer associated with DFI. This second, broad type of technology difference is modeled by assuming that production functions in the foreign investment sector and foreign sector are related by

$$f_F(e_F) = \mu f^*(e^*), \qquad e_F = e^*, \tag{9}$$

where μ measures the effect of these capital-specific differences. In this case foreign investment is stimulated, *ceteris paribus*, by larger values of μ.

For estimations we have selected as our basic production relationship a CES (constant elasticity of substitution) function of the general form

$$f^*(e^*) = A[\omega(e^*)^{-\beta} + (1 - \omega)]^{-1/\beta}, \tag{10}$$

where β is related to ρ, the constant elasticity of substitution, by $\beta = (1/\rho) - 1$, A is an appropriate scale parameter, and ω is a weighting factor for the input of capital. Note that equation (10) refers to production in the foreign sector; the other two production functions are found by a direct application of equations (8) and (9).

Finally, several comments should be added regarding the role of government policy and the nature of the foreign sector in the model. Government activity influences foreign investment in several ways. First, tax policy with respect to profits from domestic and overseas investment directly affects the global allocation of capital and alters the flow of income and savings. In addition, taxes levied on foreign investment earnings are part of the government's total tax revenues, which contribute to aggregate savings to the extent that revenues exceed government expenditure. In our estimates the level of the foreign investment tax was chosen to reflect current U.S. tax policy in which a credit is allowed for foreign taxes paid up to the full amount of the U.S. tax. In this version of the model the size of the government surplus or deficit was imbedded in our choice of aggregate savings propensity, which was based on historical values.

To reach a determinate outcome in the model, it is also necessary to specify economic behavior in the foreign sector. In this area, we have tried to strike a practical balance between realistic assumptions and the need to keep the model concise. Foreign investment earnings are assumed to be taxed abroad at a fixed proportional rate.[8] In addition, foreign hosts pursue savings policies that result in a stable long-run aggregate capital/labor ratio (i.e., the ratio of capital *owned* by foreigners to the foreign labor supply). We recognize, of course, that other assumptions—such as a fixed foreign savings propensity—are legitimate alternatives to this specification, but an assumption of the latter type leads to the unnecessary complexities of a full-fledged, two country (or multicountry) model.[9]

Finally, we have followed the neoclassical view that in the long run the current account, i.e., net exports plus net earnings on overseas investment, must be in balance with new capital outflow from additional DFI. It is possible, however, to allow for an imbalance in the steady state equilibrium by an appropriate change in the aggregate propensity to save. Any persistent deficit in this version of the "basic balance" acts as an additional source of savings to the aggregate economy.[10]

In general, the experiments that we perform below are similar to those carried out in earlier sections. In order to evaluate the effects of

[8] Our tax parameters were not set to reflect the effects of deferral of U.S. tax on income earned abroad. To the extent that deferral results in a permanent exemption from U.S. taxes, the total tax on overseas corporate profits should be somewhat lower. The reader is invited to examine the results of our sensitivity tests in Appendix E to consider what the effects of this assumption might be.

[9] Some experiments with a fixed savings rate in a two-country model indicate that approximately the same results can be obtained. Also, sensitivity tests on the choice of foreign capital/labor ratio show that our results are fairly stable over a reasonable range of values.

[10] This situation could arise, for example, if the U.S. were assigned the role of supplying transactions balances to the rest of the world, as was the case in the late fifties and sixties.

DFI, we shall compare steady states in two alternative regimes: one in which DFI is allowed, which presumably is observable, and a hypothetical regime in which DFI is prohibited. In the latter case the steady state is determined by the equation,

$$\eta k = \zeta f(k). \tag{5'}$$

Hence, in this regime the steady state income level and its distribution are computed with the value of k that satisfies (5'). (Notice that k, the *owned* capital/labor ratio, can be used as the argument of $f(\cdot)$ in this case, since foreign investment is prohibited.)

The Long-Run Effects of Direct Foreign Investment

One of the attractive features of a highly aggregated model is that it requires relatively few pieces of outside information. The other side of this advantage, however, is that results tend to depend closely on the specification of relationships and parameters. Although relatively reliable values for many of the basic parameters are available in published sources, for several others we have had to supply our own estimates. Perhaps the most uncertain are the parameters that measure the size of the technology and cost gaps across the three sectors of the global model. Since these parameters are important, inasmuch as technology differences provide the basic motive for DFI, a brief description of our method of estimation is needed.

We have proceeded by choosing parameter values for the technology and cost gaps that result in an equilibrium level of overseas investment that is in accord with observed historical levels. In doing so, we have taken note of the fact that in the early 1970s the average reported net return from foreign investment was somewhat higher than that from domestic investment.[11] Although reported foreign profits may have been somewhat inflated for tax purposes, we have assumed that foreign investors in our base year of 1970 required approximately a 25% premium on the return to foreign invested capital. (i.e., foreign investment capital must earn a return that is at least five fourths that

---

[11] Estimates of the rate of return on domestic and foreign investment vary and are uncertain due to both conceptual differences and reporting errors. We have used the figures appearing in Musgrave (1975, Chapter 10) as a best approximation.

of domestic investment). Then, relying on the fact that in 1970 the stock of foreign invested capital was approximately 6% of the total U.S. owned capital stock, we found the technology parameters that produced this capital stock ratio in the steady state.[12]

In Table 1 we present the results from three alternative experiments that measure the effect of DFI on the size and composition of national income. The estimates in column 1 are calculated on the basis of the 25% rate of return difference described above. Thus, the entries indicate in percentage terms the change in equilibrium income levels and shares that would have occurred had foreign investment been prohibited in 1970. It may be argued, however, that in 1970 the adjustment process might not yet have been completed and that with the passage of time the required premium on foreign investment earnings may have declined. Hence, these results constitute a conservative view. For comparison, therefore, we also show in columns 2 and 3, the outcome when the return differential is reduced to 15% and zero, respectively. As one would expect, the percentage changes in columns 2 and 3 are absolutely larger than corresponding entries in column 1, but are always in the same direction.

In all cases, moving to autarky produces an increase in both the real wage (row 4) and the share of national income going to labor (row 5). The rise in labor income is substantial for the experiments in columns 2 and 3, reflecting the fact that the domestic capital stock is appreciably larger in the no-DFI regime than in a regime in which DFI is permitted. Even by the relatively conservative estimates in column 1, however, wage income is increased by more than 3%. On the other hand, income accruing to capital (pre–U.S. tax, but post-foreign tax)

---

[12] The capital stock concept in this calculation is defined to include the entire privately owned capital stock of the United States, i.e., property, plant, equipment, and inventories of the corporate, unincorporated, and household sectors (excluding consumer durables). The 6% figure was derived by first using the figures for all industries in columns 2 and 4 of Table 2-4 of Musgrave (1975) for domestic and foreign fixed assets. Foreign assets were expanded by allowing 25% for foreign inventories, and domestic assets were expanded to the broader definition of capital stock by applying the proportions given in Christensen and Jorgenson (1969, p. 301). If a narrower definition of the capital stock were used (on the assumption, for example, that there is relatively little factor substitution between the corporate sector and the rest of the economy) the 6% capital stock ratio should be increased and the effect of DFI on domestic incomes in the corporate sector would be larger; the effect on incomes outside the sector of principal impact would be reduced.

TABLE 1

Comparison of long-run equilibrium values with and without direct foreign investment[a]

	(1)	(2)	(3)
1. Equilibrium ratio of foreign subsidiary capital stock to domestic capital stock	0.06	0.12	0.18
2. Change in U.S. national income	0.53%	1.40%	2.96%
3. Change in U.S. rate of return	−5.86%	−11.55%	−18.21%
4. Change in U.S. wages	3.35%	7.00%	11.96%
5. Change in labor's share of national income	1.24%	2.31%	3.42%
6. Home/foreign substitution ratio	1.13	1.17	1.21

[a] Column 1 assumes that U.S. foreign investors require a 25% premium; column 2, a 15% premium; column 3, no premium.

The comparison made in this table is between the steady state equilibrium in a no-DFI regime and that in a regime in which DFI is allowed. Changes are reported for movement to the no-DFI regime. Accordingly, entries in the table should be interpreted as follows:

row 1: $(k - e)/k$,   row 2: $[(y_0 - y)/y] \times 100$,

row 3: $[(r_0 - r)/r] \times 100$,   row 4: $[(w_0 - w)/w] \times 100$,

row 5: $[(w_0/y_0) - (w/y)] \times 100$,   row 6: $(k_0 - e)/(k - e)$,

where r, w, and y stand for domestic rate of return, wages, and per capita national income, respectively. The 0-subscript indicates steady state levels when DFI is prohibited; otherwise, variables are steady state values when DFI is allowed.

The parameter values used in results reported in this table are:

$A = 1.0$, $k^* = 3.4$, $t = 0.43$, $\eta = 0.07$,

$\theta = 0.40$, $\lambda = 0.935$, $\mu = 1.069$, $\rho = 0.75$ $(\beta = \frac{1}{3})$,

$\zeta = 0.16$, $\lambda = 0.43$, $\tau^* = 0.40$, $\omega = 0.461$.

Production parameters (A, ρ, and ω) and tax levels (τ, τ^* and t) are based on Musgrave (1975, Chapter 9). Derivation of the technology parameters (λ and μ) is described in the text. The aggregate propensity to save, ζ, is based on annual data in various issues of the *Survey of Current Business*, and includes allowance for a 2% (or GNP) government budget deficit. The 7% figure for η is based on a 6% annual depreciation rate and 1% annual growth rate of the labor force. The capital/labor ratio estimate for the foreign sector, k^*, is assumed to be 15% lower than the corresponding steady state figure for the United States. The parameter θ is intended to be a rough measure of the relative size of the foreign corporate sector(s) in DFI host countries.

declines significantly in all cases. This is hardly surprising, since the higher return abroad is presumably the original motive for DFI.

Note also that labor's *share* of income (row 5) increases less rapidly than the *level* of labor income (row 4), due to the fact that national income expands (by 0.53% in column 1) under the no DFI regime. This outcome may be somewhat surprising in light of one's usual expectation that a freer movement of factors of production should ordinarily result in a more efficient allocation of resources and higher aggregate income.

There are two reasons for this. One is the large deadweight loss to the home economy caused by tax payments to foreign treasuries. Although overseas investors care about the total tax assessed on overseas earnings, they may be presumed to be indifferent to the nationality of the tax collector. The home treasury, of course, is not. Current U.S. tax law allows a full credit for foreign taxes paid; under present foreign and domestic tax rates, the result is that over 90% of taxes paid on foreign subsidiaries' earnings go to foreign governments. In addition, since the aggregate foreign rate of return is influenced by the level of foreign investment, U.S. firms, taken collectively, may have some potential monopoly power that is not fully exploited under competitive conditions. [13]

From the equilibrium values of the model it is also possible to obtain an estimate of the long-run version of the home–foreign substitution effect referred to earlier. One measure of this is the extra capital stock that would have been retained at home had DFI been disallowed, expressed as a fraction of the actual stock of capital invested overseas. This long-run substitution ratio, shown in row 6 of Table 1, turns out to exceed 1.0 in every case. This means that in the long run, for every dollar's worth of capital stock invested overseas, more than one dollar's worth would have been invested at home had DFI been prohibited. The explanation of this somewhat counter-intuitive result is related to our earlier observation that, if DFI were not allowed, home income would rise. This increase in income would generate, in turn, extra savings and extra investment, all of which

[13] The possibility of overinvestment abroad by U.S. firms has been suggested elsewhere. See, for example, Musgrave (1975).

would be retained in the domestic economy. After all adjustments to the new steady state take place, the consequence is apparently a larger than unitary net shift in the domestic capital stock.

Distributional Effects on Savings in the DFI Model

In reaching the results of the previous section an important assumption was that the aggregate savings propensity is maintained at a constant level under the rather substantial structural changes implied by the experiment. Although Fig. 1 is not drawn to scale, it is evident from the diagram that the steady state equilibrium can be quite sensitive to our choice of aggregate savings rate. Because the lines corresponding to $G(k)$ and $\eta k/\zeta$ will ordinarily cross at a sharp angle, small changes in relative slopes will bring about a rather large shift in the position of the intersection point. This implies not only that we must be especially careful to estimate ζ (and η) accurately, but also that our results may be strongly influenced by a change in the aggregate savings propensity between the DFI regime and the regime in which DFI is prohibited.

It has been argued that an important feature of foreign investment is that it generates higher corporate profits which are, in turn, a significant source of funds for investment that would not otherwise be available. This hypothesis raises at least the possibility that if the corporate savings propensity were high enough, the distributional effects on income from encouraging DFI would induce extra aggregate saving that would offset the adverse effects described in the simpler model above. Arguing the same point in reverse, we may ask whether or not it is the case that, when foreign investment is restricted, the negative effect on corporate savings is strong enough to offset the positive effects on domestic production and tax revenues from the repatriation of capital.

To explore these issues more rigorously we have modified the simple aggregate model to reveal the effects of changes in the composition of income on the structure of savings. Equation (5) is now replaced by

$$\eta k = s, \tag{11}$$

and per capita savings s is disaggregated by sectors as follows:

$$s = s_h + s_c + s_g + s_f, \qquad (12)$$

$$\begin{aligned} s_h = \zeta_h(1 - t_h)\{w &+ [(1 - \pi)[[(1 - \tau)(r - \delta)e] \\ &+ [(1 - \pi_F)(1 - t)(r_F - \delta)(k - e)]]]\}, \end{aligned} \qquad (13)$$

$$\begin{aligned} s_c = (\delta k) &+ \{\pi[[(1 - \tau)(r - \delta)e] \\ &+ [(1 - \pi_F)(1 - t)(r_F - \delta)(k - e)]]\} \\ &+ [\pi_F(1 - t)(r_F - \delta)(k - e)], \end{aligned} \qquad (14)$$

$$\begin{aligned} s_g = \zeta_g\{[(t_h s_h)/[\sigma_h(1 - t_h)]] &+ [\tau(r - \delta)e] \\ &+ [(t - \tau^*)(r_F - \delta)(k - e)]\}, \end{aligned} \qquad (15)$$

$$s_f = \zeta_f[f(e)], \qquad (16)$$

where:

s_h is household savings per capita,
s_c corporate savings per capita,
s_g the government surplus per capita,
s_f the per capita deficit in the "basic balance" (as used in the text),
ζ_h the household savings propensity (constant),
ζ_g the government savings propensity (constant),
ζ_f the foreign sector savings propensity (constant),
π the share of domestic after-tax profits retained by the corporate sector (constant),
π_F the share of foreign source profits retained by corporations in the foreign investment sector (constant),
δ the percentage annual depreciation allowance (constant),
t_h the tax rate on household income (constant),
r the home rate of return to capital (equal to $f'(e)$),
r_F the rate of return in the foreign investment sector (equal to $f'_F(e_F)$),
w the domestic wage (equal to $f(e) - ef'(e)$).

Equation (13) requires that household saving be a constant fraction of disposable income, inclusive of distributed corporate profits. In equation (14) corporate savings is controlled by the two parameters, π and π_F, that describe corporate dividend policy. Notice that gross retentions in (14) include a nontaxed allowance for depreciation of capital. Government saving in (15) is assumed to be a stable share of total revenues, and saving from external transactions in (16) stands in a fixed ratio to domestic production.

The disaggregated system of equations (1)–(4) and (11)–(16) has ten variables—k, e, e_F, e^*, ψ, s, s_h, s_c, s_g, and s_f—and may be solved for steady state, equilibrium values in the same fashion as in the previous version of the model. Equilibrium values can then be compared to those from a corresponding no-DFI equilibrium that is defined by the following modified system of equations:

$$\eta k = s \tag{11}$$

$$s = s_h + s_c + s_g + s_f \tag{12}$$

$$s_h = \zeta_h (1 - t_h)\{w + [(1 - \pi)(1 - \tau)(r - \delta)k]\} \tag{13'}$$

$$s_c = (\delta k) + [\pi(1 - \tau)(r - \delta)k] \tag{14'}$$

$$s_g = \zeta_g/\{[(t_h s_h)/[\sigma_h(1 - t_h)]] + [\tau(r - \delta)k]\} \tag{15'}$$

$$s_f = \zeta_f[f(k)] \tag{16'}$$

In Table 2 we report results analogous to those in Table 1 from a simulation with this model, using historical estimates of the additional necessary parameters. Since we are interested here in the effects of DFI on sectoral savings, we have also added to the table the results of several sensitivity tests on sectoral-specific savings propensities. The results reveal that distributional effects on savings can have a very powerful influence on the long-run equilibrium. In fact, in column 1, using our "best estimate" base values, the previous conclusions about the effect of DFI on incomes are reversed. This experiment suggests that, if DFI were prohibited, long-run U.S. national income would be as much as 3% *lower*, while wages and the return to capital would be about 1.5% lower and 3% higher, respectively. This turnabout is due in large part to the depressing effect on corporate savings and aggregate capital formation caused by shifting away from foreign investment. One measure of this decline in capital formation is the home–foreign substitution ratio in row 6. Still referring to the basic simulation in column 1 of Table 2, the value of -0.50 indicates that under the assumptions of this exercise for every unit of foreign-invested capital returned home, about one-half unit *less* is eventually operating at home

TABLE 2

Comparison of long-run equilibrium values with disaggregated savings[a]

	(1) Base values	(2) $\Delta \zeta_\eta$	(3) $\Delta \pi$	(4) $\Delta \pi_F$	(5) $\Delta \zeta_g$
1. Equilibrium ratio of foreign subsidiary capital stock to domestic capital stock	0.06	0.06	0.06	0.06	0.06
2. Change in U.S. national income	−3.00 %[b]	−3.04 %	−3.21 %	−3.23 %	−3.14 %
3. Change in U.S. rate of return	2.88 %	2.99 %	3.43 %	3.46 %	3.18 %
4. Change in U.S. wages	−1.51 %	−1.56 %	−1.79 %	−1.80 %	−1.67 %
5. Change in labor's share of national income	1.23 %	1.23 %	1.24 %	1.24 %	1.24 %
6. Home/foreign substitution ratio	−0.50	−0.52	−0.59	−0.60	−0.55

[a] Base values are the same as those given in Table 1, plus the following:

$t_h = 0.20$, $\delta = 0.05$, $\pi = 0.40$, $\pi_F = 0.0$,

$\zeta_f = 0.0$, $\zeta_g = -0.27$ $\zeta_h = 0.10$.

(Notice that $\pi_F = 0.0$ implies that all foreign earned profits are assumed to be distributed to the domestic parent before ultimate distribution to the public, as determined by π.) Entries in row 1–6 of this table correspond to those in Table 1; for interpretation, see footnote to Table 1. The sensitivity tests in columns 2–5 of this table make the following parameter changes:

column 2: $\zeta_h = 0.11$ $(\Delta\zeta_h/\zeta_h = 10\%)$,   column 3: $\pi = 0.44$ $(\Delta\pi/\pi = 10\%)$,

column 4: $\pi_F = 0.02$,   column 5: $\zeta_g = -0.274$ $(\Delta\zeta_g/\zeta_g = 2\%)$.

[b] In the same experiment steady state consumption per capita declines by slightly over 2 % when DFI is prohibited.

in the long-run equilibrium. Interestingly, labor's share of total national income still increases slightly, although in this case the rise occurs because wages fall less rapidly than income.

In interpreting these findings one should not make the mistake of concluding that, because there is more structural detail in this version of the model, that its results are necessarily superior. In fact, there are reasons to believe that the opposite may be the case. The results of the sensitivity tests in columns 2–5 of Table 2 suggest that the outcome can be strongly affected by the levels of the savings parameters—in particular, parameters such as π_F and to a lesser degree π and ζ_g, which influence the DFI and no-DFI equilibria in a differential fashion. A similar strong effect would presumably be seen if we allowed ζ_f to change when shifting between regimes.

This exercise apparently suffers from limitations similar to those of the previous model, although at a more refined level. We are requiring, in effect, that certain behavioral relationships be rigidly maintained in the face of broad shifts in the underlying structure of the economy. In particular, it may be straining credibility to suppose that policies affecting corporate and government savings would remain neutral (in the sense of unchanged savings propensities) under these circumstances. Even under a less extreme shift than outright prohibition of DFI, it is one thing to assume a stable household savings propensity, but quite another to require that corporations continue to pay out dividends at an unchanged rate and reduce net investment to the extent that the home–foreign substitution ratio turns negative. What would actually happen to corporate savings if DFI were restricted is a behavioral and empirical question that we are not in a good position to answer. Likewise, we cannot know at this point whether fiscal policy would be used in these circumstances to fill any savings gap that might emerge. It is important to point out, however, that if this were the case, the outcome would be closer to that of the simpler, aggregate model.

The results in this section are somewhat less than fully satisfying, inasmuch as they suggest how difficult it is to pin down even the direction of change of long-run incomes. However, in spite of the uncertainty of our estimates, the analysis does have an important message, namely, that the effect of DFI on long-run income and its distribution is strongly influenced by corollary effects on savings. Although the results that we presented in Table 1, column 1, as the distributional effects of DFI are in broad agreement with other published estimates, it should now be apparent that these depend quite closely on specific assumptions about the behavior of aggregate savings. As the more detailed model reveals, it is quite easy to generate a distinctly different outcome with only small changes in assumptions. In view of this sensitivity, policy makers in this area should be alert to these possibilities to insure that the intended effect of a policy shift is not weakened or even reversed. Moreover, the fact that increased savings from distributional effects may produce increases in long-run national income should not be interpreted as an argument in favor of such shifts; surely, there are other more direct ways of stimulating domestic savings that can accomplish the same result without imposing such a heavy burden on domestic labor.

Direct Technology Transfer in a Long-Run Model

In this section we shall modify the DFI model of the previous sections to consider the long-run consequences of direct technology transfers without associated capital flow. In effect, we ask the hypothetical question; what would be the implications for U.S. income and its distribution if U.S. firms transferred technology exclusively by means of licensing arrangements?

The analysis is carried out at a comparable level of aggregation and is similar in most respects to that of the preceding sections. It differs, however, in that we assume here that U.S. firms relinquish control over some part of their transferable technological advantages (i.e., those of the capital-specific type) to foreign firms in return for a royalty payment levied on foreign production. We shall continue to rely on the technology gap estimates obtained earlier, but it is recognized that without associated capital flow not all of the measured gap may be transferable to the foreign site through licensing. Some aspects of the technology advantage are likely to be highly specific to the firm of origin and may require the immediate presence of U.S. ownership and managerial skills. To reflect this limitation, we have modified the technological coefficients in the recipient foreign sector by a parameter that measures the degree to which the technology transfer is effected. In the estimates below, we have traced out results in each instance for a high (100%), middle (70%), and low (30%) degree of transfer.

Also, since it is not practical, particularly at this level of aggregation, to specify with any detail the international market for technological information and skills, we have followed a similar procedure in setting the average per unit royalty rate. The theoretical maximum royalty is that which would leave a foreign producer indifferent between entering the licensing agreement or using inferior local production techniques. We have experimented with three values that span the possible range of royalties—with the high, middle, and low levels corresponding to 85, 50, and 15% of this maximum level, respectively.

Finally, in order to make an appropriate comparison with the previous analysis of DFI, we have assumed that U.S. producers will choose to produce at home the same share of total U.S. technology product (i.e., U.S. domestic production plus the production of either U.S. subsidiaries or licensed foreign firms) in the direct transfer case as in the case of transfer through foreign investment.[14] This assumption implies, of course, that in these experiments production by licensed foreign firms substitutes directly for production by foreign subsidiaries.

The revised model uses the following relationships:

$$e = k, \tag{17}$$

$$k^* = \phi e_0^* + (1 - \phi)e_z^*, \tag{18}$$

$$f^*(e^*) - e^* f^{*\prime}(e^*) = f_z^*(e_z^*) - e_z^* f_z^{*\prime}(e_z^*), \tag{19}$$

$$m = \theta f(e)/[\theta f(e) + f_z^*(e_z^*)(1 - \phi)(1 - \theta)], \tag{20}$$

$$\eta k = \zeta[f(e) + [z f_z^*(e_z^*)](1 - \phi)(1 - \theta)/\theta], \tag{21}$$

$$f_z^*(e_z^*) = v\mu f^*(e^*), \qquad e_z^* = e^*, \tag{22}$$

$$f(e) = \lambda f_z^*(e^*), \qquad e^* = e, \tag{23}$$

where

z is the per unit royalty (constant),
v measures the effectiveness of technology transfer (constant),
ϕ measures the share of the foreign labor supply employed in the sector of the foreign country not using imported technology,
m is the home country's market share of total U.S.-technology product (constant),

and where the subscript z indicates variables in the foreign sector that employs licensed technology.

Once again, there are three aggregate production sectors in the model—a domestic sector, a local-technology foreign sector, and a

---

[14] This parameter's value is obtained from the experiment of column 1, Table 1. This assumption might be justified by appeal, for example, to a constant market share strategy on the part of U.S. producers. Alternative assumptions are, of course, possible.

foreign sector that uses imported technology. The latter, in effect, replaces the DFI sector of the previous models.

Equations (17) and (18) are full-employment conditions, analogous to equations (1) and (2) of the DFI model. Notice, however, that the specification of (17) and (18) implies that net international capital flow is zero. Equation (19) sets the common wage for the two foreign production sectors. Our market-share assumption is embodied in equation (20). The steady state level of k is determined by equation (21); national income in this case includes royalties earned on licensed technology. Equations (22) and (23) are the counterparts of equations (8) and (9); equation (22) reflects our assumptions about the degree of effectiveness of technology transfer through the use of the parameter v.

The outcome of a series of experiments over the range of both royalty levels and degree of effective transfer are presented in Table 3. In each case, percentage changes in variables (or changes in percentage shares) are shown using autarky (i.e., no technology transfer) as the standard of comparison. Since the same base and parameters were used in Table 1, these new figures may be compared directly with the earlier results.

The entries in Table 3 suggest that an exclusive system of direct technology transfer would have a relatively small impact on U.S. income and its components when compared to the autarky position. In only two cases are the effects on national income greater than a 1.0% change. However, inasmuch as the directions of national income and wage changes in Table 3 are opposite to those of Table 1, the net effect of a shift from DFI to licensing would be more substantial. Taking the strongest case in Table 3 (row 1) together with the entries in column 1 of Table 1, they suggest that a shift from DFI to licensing would raise national income by more than 2%, reduce the average return to capital by about 4%, and raise wages by about 4% in the long run.

It should be recalled that technology transfer without any associated capital flow permits investors (that is, those in a position to earn a return from control over capital and technology) to capture only the quasi rent associated with transferable, capital-specific advantages (and then, only part of that quasi rent, depending on assumptions about the degree of transfer and size of the royalty). Access to labor-specific technological factors associated with production abroad are not

TABLE 3

Comparison of long-run equilibrium values with and without direct technology transfer[a]

	(1) Change in U.S. national income (%)	(2) Change in U.S. average rate of return (%)	(3) Change in U.S. wages (%)	(4) Change in labor's share of national income (%)
$v = 1.0$ (full transfer)				
z = high value (85%)	−1.55	−1.72	−0.67	0.57
z = mid value (50%)	−0.91	−1.01	−0.40	0.34
z = low value (15%)	−0.28	−0.31	−0.12	0.10
$v = 0.981$ (70% transfer)				
z = high value (85%)	−1.11	−1.21	−0.50	0.41
z = mid value (50%)	−0.66	−0.72	−0.29	0.24
z = low value (15%)	−0.20	−0.22	−0.09	0.07
$v = 0.955$ (30% transfer)				
z = high value (85%)	−0.49	−0.53	−0.22	0.18
z = mid value (50%)	−0.29	−0.31	−0.13	0.11
z = low value (15%)	−0.09	−0.09	−0.04	0.03

[a] The comparisons made in this table are between steady state levels under a no-transfer regime (autarky) and a regime with direct technology transfer and royalty payments, as indicated. Entries should be interpreted as follows:

column 1: $[(y_0 - y)/y] \times 100$,   column 2: $[(r_0 - r)/r] \times 100$,
column 3: $[(w_0 - w)/w] \times 100$,   column 4: $[(w_0/y_0) - (w/y)] \times 100$.

Again, the 0-subscript indicates steady state values. National income in the regime with transfers, y, includes royalties. The domestic rate of return in this regime is an average rate and includes a prorated share of royalty payments, that is,

$$r = \{[f(e) + [z/_z^*](e_z^*)](1 - \theta)(1 - \phi)/\theta] - w\}/e.$$

Parameter values, including those for λ and μ, are the same as those used in Table 1, column 1.

available to home investors under the licensing assumption. Still, it appears that any returns foregone by licensing are more than offset by the retention of tax revenues that would be lost under DFI. It is also worth pointing out that in Table 3 the separate contribution to distributional changes attributable to the shift to licensing (from autarky) is relatively mild, primarily because licensing does not involve any relocation of domestic capital.

Summary

Several points emerge from the analysis of this chapter. First, the findings suggest that, if we assume an unchanged aggregate savings rate, foreign investment has brought about a moderate decline in both wage rates and labor's share of national income. There also appears to have been a slight overall loss in total income accruing to the U.S. economy under the current tax system, primarily because of large tax payments on foreign earnings that are collected by foreign treasuries. This implies that additional restrictions on U.S. overseas investment, for example, in the form of a higher domestic tax on foreign earnings, could yield an increase in long-run per capita income. This conclusion, however, is very sensitive to the assumption of an unchanged savings propensity—a point on which we need not elaborate again.

A shift toward direct transfer of technology through licensing provides an alternative method of bypassing these tax payments and reducing this loss. Our results show that direct transfers would produce small increases in national income, as well as increases in property income and labor income components. These gains are constrained, however, by the degree to which technology can be effectively transferred and by the size of the royalty that can be extracted from foreign users.

It is important to reemphasize that the estimates we have made in this chapter are inevitably imperfect, and that at this point should be treated as no more than tentative measures of the scale and direction of these effects. In this regard, the practical limitations of general equilibrium models and the *caveats* that apply to the use of neoclassical assumptions should be kept well in mind. We have also added several assumptions of our own to the analysis that undoubtedly influence the outcome. For example, the results are strongly affected by our definition of the capital stock, which in turn controls the specification of the aggregate production function and its parameters. Moreover, we have relied on very strong *ceteris paribus* assumptions in order to focus attention on the role of foreign investment and technology— thereby ignoring a number of potentially important related issues, including induced balance of payments disequilibria, reverse investment flows, production of new technological capability through research and development, and changes in market structure over time.

The results of the sensitivity tests (shown in 1 and 2 of Appendix E) are worth brief comment in this regard since they give some indication of how these conclusions would be affected by changes in the basic parameters of the model. On balance, the results based on comparisons of steady states are relatively stable over changes in the model's parameters. The steady states themselves, however, can be quite sensitive to changes in savings rates, growth rates, and the technology gap parameters, in particular. Accordingly, one of the least satisfactory aspects of this type of exercise is the need to solve out the system for the parameters that measure technology gaps. Although the estimates are plausible (they are roughly 7% in the basic model), a reliable, independent estimate would be a very useful additional input. Current information, however, is not of sufficient quality to support direct attempt to measure these gaps. This suggests, of course, the need for further refinement of the production and capital stock data in this area as a precondition for further, more detailed research.

Chapter IX

Concluding Remarks

In our study we have examined the effect of U.S. direct foreign investment on domestic employment in the short run and on the size and composition of domestic income in the long run. The analytical models we have employed for these purposes—the short-run model developed in Chapter III and the long-run model developed in Chapter VIII—differ markedly in their characterizations of the U.S. foreign investment program. Here we comment briefly on these differences and on some of the policy questions for which these models may be relevant.

The explicit focus of the short-run micro model of Chapter III is the behavior of individual multinational firms. We attempted to answer the specific question of how short-run domestic employment demand would have differed for a given firm had that firm been denied the option of investing abroad. In approaching that question we disregarded the supply side of the labor market, assuming that layoffs or hours variations, rather than wage variations, are the predominant short-run manifestation of shifts in final product demand. Our short-run model also ignored the effect of capital outflows on the size of the domestic capital stock and, in turn, made no attempt to specify the long-run influence of this stock on domestic employment demands.

On the basis of very crude data on demand and cost conditions, we calculated that, though U.S. multinationals possess a certain degree of market power in the final product markets served by their subsidiaries abroad, such enterprises would nonetheless lose the lion's share of those markets if they attempted to serve them by exporting from the U.S. We also observed, however, that the number of domestic jobs whose existence can be attributed to the current operations of overseas subsidiaries is not large. The number of such jobs is so small, in fact, that domestic employment demands would be somewhat higher in the short run in a hypothetical regime that denied the option of foreign subsidiary production.

In the context of our long-run model, the question of what individual firms would do in the absence of a direct foreign investment alternative simply does not arise. It is assumed in this model that natural equilibrating tendencies and/or policy intervention act to maintain full employment along a steady state growth path. In the basic version of this model, the principal consequences of an ongoing foreign investment program are that the size of the domestic capital stock is reduced and that much of the income generated by U.S. owned capital abroad accrues in the form of corporate tax payments to host country treasuries. In the process, U.S. domestic income (net of foreign tax payments) declines, as do both the share and absolute size of income that accrues to U.S. labor. The income of U.S. capital ownership (net of all taxes) was seen to increase in the long-run model, a less than surprising conclusion since higher rates of return abroad were assumed to be the motivating factor behind direct foreign investment in the first place.

In a more disaggregated version of the long-run model in which the savings rate for the corporate sector was assumed to be higher than for other sectors, the increase in corporate income from DFI generated a higher level of savings for the economy. This savings increase, in turn, served to increase domestic income (and consumption) by amounts sufficient to offset the revenues lost to foreign treasuries. We cautioned, however, that there is no evidence that redistribution of income in favor of the corporate sector would actually produce the hypothesized increase in aggregate savings. We also pointed out that if large gains would indeed result from increased national savings, there are more equitable and efficient means of achieving this result than the transfer of income from other sectors to the corporate sector.

At numerous junctures we have stressed that the estimates constructed in our study should be regarded primarily as illustrative in character. For the sake of discussion, however, let us now assume that the signs, if not the magnitudes, of these estimates are correct. What policy implications follow from such an assumption?

First, the estimates from our short-run model suggest that domestic labor market displacements do occur in response to U.S. direct foreign investment, a conclusion at odds with most of the literature on this subject reviewed in Chapter II. However, the share of our current unemployment that can be attributed to direct foreign investment was seen in Chapter VII to be relatively small. If the benefits of the foreign investment program were sufficiently large, therefore, they would warrant continuation of the program in combination with policies designed to ease the specific domestic burdens that foreign investment creates.

The estimates from our long-run model suggest, however, that the U.S. foreign investment program, far from producing large benefits, may actually depress the long-run path of domestic income below that which would have obtained in a regime without direct foreign investment.

Do these estimates point to the need for a national policy whose aim is to curtail U.S. direct foreign investment? Before presuming that they do, a number of important issues must be considered.

First, we should stress that our long-run model does not conflict, as it may appear to, with the traditional notion that overall output levels rise when factors of production are permitted to move more freely across arbitrary national boundaries. While U.S. domestic income (including post–foreign tax return from U.S. direct investment capital) is lower than it would have been in a no-DFI regime, the comparison of *world* output between the two regimes goes in the opposite direction— the loss in U.S. income is more than made up for by the gain in host country revenues from taxes paid by the U.S. multinationals and the higher host country labor incomes associated with the presence of U.S. owned capital. Rather than eliminate activities that increase world output, both the United States and the host country would profit by negotiating systems of transfers that enable both parties to share in the fruits of those activities.[1]

A far more important consideration is that all of our analysis has looked at the U.S. foreign investment program in isolation from the investment programs of multinationals headquartered in other nations. For the period to which our data pertain—the late sixties and early seventies—this focus is appropriate because U.S. capital outflows then vastly exceed the flow of direct investment capital into the United States. In more recent years, however, inflows have become significantly larger.

All of our arguments about the effects of U.S. capital outflows on the domestic economy apply in reverse concerning the effects of foreign capital movements into the United States. U.S. labor is the clear beneficiary of such inflows, as is the U.S. Treasury, while the position of U.S. capital owners is weakened by them. To the extent that the stock of foreign capital in place in the United States may soon approach in size the stock of U.S. capital abroad, the gains and losses will tend to offset one another and both the United States and other investing countries will claim their fair shares of the overall gains produced by international capital movements.

In the meantime, a movement to restrict U.S. capital from flowing abroad[2] would invite foreign governments to retaliate by restricting the flow of foreign capital into the United States. The ultimate result of mutual restrictions of this sort would, of course, be that all parties suffer a decline in economic well-being.

The principal policy conclusion of our study is thus a rather negative one; we simply do not know enough about the domestic repurcussions of U.S. direct foreign investment to justify a program of policy intervention for or against it. In particular, we stress our belief that none of the estimates in our study establishes a clear case for

[1] In the case of foreign investment in less developed countries, the U.S. position might be to forgo such transfers in the interest of promoting host country economic growth. It should be kept in mind, however, that most U.S. direct foreign investment capital is concentrated not in less developed countries, but in the highly industrialized and prosperous nations of Western Europe and Canada.

[2] The question has been raised of whether techniques even exist that are capable of preventing such capital outflows as long as multinationals are free to choose the countries in which their headquarters are located (see Harberger, 1978).

policy measures that attempt to prohibit the outflow of U.S. direct investment capital. On the other hand, it is worth noting that much of our current tax policy toward U.S. multinationals was enacted during a period in which the presumption of law makers appears to have been that capital outflows have an unambiguously beneficial effect on all sectors of the domestic economy, a characterization that our estimates do not support. For example, the current policy of deferring taxation of multinationals' subsidiary earnings provides an incentive beyond that which the market itself provides for U.S. firms to increase their capital stocks abroad. We have argued elsewhere[3] that tax policies of this sort are difficult to defend in cases where capital outflows impose significant costs on certain sectors of the domestic economy.

As more and better data accumulate we hope that some of the methods we have developed in this study can be used to generate a clearer picture of how foreign investment affects the domestic economy. In the meantime, as crude and tentative as the estimates of our study are, they do suggest, we believe, that tax policies whose aim or effect is to encourage U.S. direct foreign investment deserve careful reevaluation.

---

[3] See Frank and Freeman (1978).

Appendix A

Details on Calculation of σ Values

Our basic approach has been to gather direct measures where possible and to construct indirect measures when necessary of the individual components in the expression for σ presented in equation (7) of Chapter III,

$$\sigma = \left(\frac{MC_F}{MC_H(1 + t)}\right)^{\eta}.$$

Marginal Cost Ratios

Foreign subsidiary income statements by industry division are available in the 1970 Department of Commerce *Special Survey of U.S. MNCs.*[1] These income statements contain no measures of marginal costs per se, but do present information which facilitates the division

[1] See U.S. Department of Commerce (1970).

of total costs by industry into fixed and variable cost categories. If production takes place under conditions of constant marginal costs, the ratio of marginal costs in two production sites may be approximated as the ratio of total variable costs in the two sites provided they are operating at the same output level. Total variable costs for the foreign site can be measured directly from the subsidiary income statements. In constructing a measure of the TVC for producing the same level of output in a hypothetical home site, we first assume that intermediate products are purchased in a world market at international prices.[2] Relying again on our previous assumption that the subsidiary duplicates its parent's technology, the materials components of home site TVC is then assigned the value of total nonlabor variable cost (TVMC), taken from the foreign subsidiary income statement.

The labor component of total variable costs is permitted to differ between sites because of differences in home and foreign unit labor costs. Thus, the hypothetical home site variable labor costs are calculated as $(\text{TVLC}_F \times r)$, where r is an estimate of the home–foreign unit labor cost ratio taken from the U.S. Tariff Commission report cited earlier and TVLC_F is the labor component of total variable costs reported in the subsidiary income statements. Finally, we calculate marginal cost ratios by industry using the formula

$$\frac{\text{MC}_F}{\text{MC}_H} = \frac{\text{TVC}_F}{(\text{TVLC}_F \times r) + \text{TVMC}_H}. \tag{1}$$

The resultant marginal cost ratios are reproduced in column 1 of Table 1 in Chapter III.

Demand Elasticity

The term η in our expression for the home–foreign substitution parameter calls for the demand elasticity facing individual firms in an industry, as opposed to an industry-wide elasticity. Though our data pertain to very crude levels of industry aggregation, if one is willing to

---

[2] Alternatively, one may assume that the MNC accomplishes the same result by manipulation of transfer prices. When this is not the case, of course, a measure of the *effective* rate of protection must be used in the expression at the top of the page.

accept profit maximization as the proximate objective of firms, the aggregative figures for revenues and costs which appear in the subsidiary income statements may be employed to infer values of demand elasticities perceived by individual firms.

For example, if η_{ij} denotes the price elasticity of demand facing the ith firm in the jth industry, the profit maximization assumption implies

$$\eta_{ij} = \frac{P_{ij}/MC_{ij}}{P_{ij}/MC_{ij} - 1}, \tag{2}$$

where P_{ij} is output price, and MC_{ij} is marginal production cost. If production is again characterized as occurring under conditions of constant marginal cost, i.e., if firm cost curves are represented as

$$TC_{ij} = FC_{ij} + MC_{ij} \times Q_{ij}, \tag{3}$$

where TC_{ij} are the total production costs, FC_{ij} the fixed production costs, and Q_{ij} the output level, then expression (2) may be conveniently recast as

$$\eta_{ij} = \frac{R_{ij}}{R_{ij} - V_{ij}}, \tag{4}$$

where R_{ij} are the total revenues, and V_{ij} the variable costs. Finally, if the demand elasticities facing firms within an industry are approximately the same (i.e., if $\eta_{ij} = \bar{\eta}_j$ for all i), then the firm demand elasticities may be expressed as

$$\bar{\eta}_j = \sum_{i=1}^{N_j} \frac{\eta_{ij}}{N_j} = \frac{1}{N_j} \sum_{i=1}^{N_j} \left(\frac{R_{ij}}{R_{ij} - V_{ij}} \right), \tag{5}$$

where N_j is the number of firms in industry j. When $(R_{ij})/(R_{ij} - V_{ij})$ is the same for each value of i, (5) reduces to[3]

$$\frac{1}{N_j} \times N_j \frac{\sum_{i=1}^{N_j} R_{ij}}{\sum_{i=1}^{N_j} (R_{ij} - V_{ij})} = \frac{R_j}{R_j - V_j}, \tag{6}$$

where R_j are the total revenues for industry j, V_j the variable costs for industry j.

---

[3] Suits has employed essentially the same procedures for estimating the domestic price elasticity of demand for firms in U.S. industries. See Suits (1970, p. 335).

These industry total revenue and variable cost measures may then be taken directly from the subsidiary income statements. Our estimates of subsidiary firm demand elasticities by industry, calculated using (6), are presented in column 2 of Table 1 in Chapter III.

Transport and Tariff Costs

As an estimate of transport, handling, storage, and insurance costs we have calculated the ratio of the c.i.f. values of imports into a region from the United States to the f.o.b. value of exports from the United States to that region. Using data published in the *United Nations Statistical Yearbook* (1970). and in the 1967 Supplement to the 1967 *Yearbook*, these ratios were calculated for Canada, the EEC, and Japan. An overall transport cost ratio was then calculated as a weighted average of these cost ratios, where the weights are the regional shares of total subsidiary capital stocks. This calculation produced the result that transport costs amount, on average, to slightly more than 13% of the value of goods shipped in 1970. The crudeness of this calculation stands out even among the other rather inelegant computations of this appendix. In computing the values of the substitution parameters, therefore, we have allowed for transport costs to range between 5% and 30% of the value of shipments.

Average tariff rates for all countries were taken for each industry group from the GATT's *Basic Documentation for Tariff Study*, Summary Table No. 2 (Contracting Parties to the General Agreement on Tariff and Trade, 1970). These tariff rates are added to the transportation cost to form the loading factor t_i which is reproduced in column 3 of Table 1 in Chapter III.

Finally, our estimates of σ for each industry were then calculated as

$$\sigma_i = \left[\frac{MC_{Fi}}{MC_{Hi}(1 + t_i)} \right]^{\eta_i}.$$

These are reproduced as column 4 in Table 1 in Chapter III. Columns 5 and 6 of the same table present the range of σ values produced as transport costs vary from 5% to 30% of the value of shipments.

Appendix B

Technical Proofs

In this brief appendix we justify several of the results that were shown in Chapter IV without proof. To obtain equation (7) of Chapter IV, we use the requirement that marginal revenue equals marginal cost in each location and the fact that quantity supplied must equal the quantity demanded at *both point A and point B*. This means that at point A

$$Z_{\text{H}}(\text{MC}_A)^\varepsilon = k(\text{MR}_A)^{-\eta} = k(\text{MC}_A)^{-\eta}, \tag{1}$$

where $k = N(1 - 1/\eta)^\eta$. Solving this relationship for the marginal cost at A we obtain

$$\text{MC}_A = k^{1/(\eta + \varepsilon)} Z_{\text{H}}^{-1/(\eta + \varepsilon)}. \tag{2}$$

Similarly, at point B the requirement that total supply equals demand means that

$$Z_{\text{H}}(\text{MC}_B)^\varepsilon + Z_{\text{F}}(\text{MC}_B)^\varepsilon = k(\text{MR}_B)^{-\eta} = k(\text{MC}_B)^{-\eta}. \tag{3}$$

Again, solving this relationship for the marginal cost, we obtain

$$MC_B = k^{1/(\varepsilon + \eta)}(Z_H + Z_F)^{-1/(\varepsilon + \eta)}. \tag{4}$$

Since the ratio Z_F/Z_H must equal μ, where μ is the market share parameter, we can substitute in (4) to obtain

$$MC_B = k^{1/(\varepsilon + \eta)}(Z_H(1 + \mu))^{-1/(\varepsilon + \eta)}. \tag{5}$$

Finally, since the proper measure for σ in this case is

$$\sigma = \frac{Q_{H_A} - Q_{H_B}}{Q_{F_B}},$$

this can be rewritten as

$$\sigma = \frac{1}{\mu}\left[\left(\frac{MC_{H_A}}{MC_{H_B}}\right)^{\varepsilon} - 1\right],$$

which is equation (IV.6). Substituting the results from (2) and (5) above, we obtain the desired relationship, namely,

$$\sigma = \frac{1}{\mu}[(1 + \mu)^{\varepsilon/(\varepsilon + \eta)} - 1]. \tag{6}$$

To obtain equation (IV.8) the procedure is similar, except that we must now take into account the fact that marginal revenue is no longer set equal to marginal cost in each location. However, using equation set (IV.5) we can write

$$MC_{H_A} = \frac{MR_A}{1 + t}, \tag{7a}$$

$$MC_{H_B} = MR_B\left[\frac{1 - T(\mu/(1 + \mu))}{1 + t}\right] = \left[\frac{(1 + \mu) - T\mu}{(1 + t)(1 + \mu)}\right], \tag{7b}$$

$$MC_{F_B} = MR_B\left[\frac{(1 + t) + T(1/(\mu + 1))}{1 + t}\right] = \left[\frac{(1 + t)(1 + \mu) + T}{(1 + t)(1 + \mu)}\right]. \tag{7c}$$

These relationships can be substituted into the supply–demand equations, (1) and (3), to obtain

$$Z_H(MC_{H_A})^{\varepsilon} = k[(1 + t)MC_{H_A}]^{-\eta} \tag{8}$$

for values at point A, and

$$Z_H (MC_{H_B})^\varepsilon + Z_F \left[\frac{(1 + t)(1 + \mu) + T}{(1 + \mu) - T\mu} \right]^\varepsilon (MC_{H_B})^\varepsilon$$

$$= k \left[\frac{(1 + t)(1 + \mu)}{(1 + \mu) - T\mu} \right]^{-\eta} (MC_{H_B})^{-\eta} \qquad (9)$$

for values at point B. Solving in each case for equilibrium values of marginal cost we obtain

$$MC_{H_A} = k^{1/(\eta + \varepsilon)} Z_H^{-1/(\eta + \varepsilon)} (1 + t)^{-\eta/(\eta + \varepsilon)}, \qquad (10)$$

$$MC_{H_B} = k^{1/(\varepsilon + \eta)} Z_H^{-1/(\varepsilon + \eta)} (1 + \mu)^{-1/(\varepsilon + \eta)} \left[\frac{(1 + t)(1 + \mu)}{(1 + \mu) - T\mu} \right]^{-\eta/(\varepsilon + \eta)}. \qquad (11)$$

By dividing (10) by (11) we obtain

$$\frac{MC_{H_A}}{MC_{H_B}} = \frac{(1 + \mu)^{(1 + \eta)/(\varepsilon + \eta)}}{(1 + \mu - \mu T)^{\eta/(\eta + \varepsilon)}},$$

which when substituted into (IV.6), yields the desired result, equation (IV.11),

$$\sigma = \frac{1}{\mu} \left[\frac{(1 + \mu)^{(\varepsilon + \eta \varepsilon)/(\eta + \varepsilon)}}{(1 + \mu - \mu T)^{\eta \varepsilon/(\eta + \varepsilon)}} - 1 \right].$$

The derivation for the tax case is quite similar except that marginal cost–marginal revenue relationships must be altered to

$$MC_{H_A} = MR_A, \qquad (12a)$$

$$MC_{H_B} = MR_B \left[1 - G \frac{\mu}{1 + \mu} \right] = MR_B \left[\frac{1 + \mu - G\mu}{1 + \mu} \right], \qquad (12b)$$

$$MC_{F_B} = MR_B \left[1 - G^* \frac{1}{1 + \mu} \right] = MR_B \left[\frac{1 + \mu - G^*}{1 + \mu} \right], \qquad (12c)$$

where

$$G = \left(\frac{t_H - t_F}{1 - t_H} \right) \left(\frac{1}{\eta - 1} \right) \quad \text{and} \quad G^* = \left(\frac{t_F - t_H}{1 - t_F} \right) \left(\frac{1}{\eta - 1} \right).$$

Solving for the marginal cost yields

$$MC_{H_A} = k^{1/(\eta + \varepsilon)} Z_H^{-1/(\eta + \varepsilon)}, \tag{13}$$

and

$$MC_{H_B} = k^{1/(\varepsilon + \eta)} Z_H^{-1/(\varepsilon + \eta)} (1 + \mu)^{-1/(\varepsilon + \eta)} \left[\frac{1 + \mu}{1 + \mu - G\mu} \right]. \tag{14}$$

Forming the ratio of the two marginal costs we obtain

$$\frac{MC_{H_A}}{MC_{H_B}} = \frac{(1 + \mu)^{(1 + \eta)/(\varepsilon + \eta)}}{(1 + \mu - \mu G)^{\eta/(\varepsilon + \eta)}}. \tag{15}$$

This can then be substituted into (IV.6) to produce equation (IV.11),

$$\sigma = \frac{1}{\mu} \left[\frac{(1 + \mu)^{(\varepsilon + \eta)/(\varepsilon + \eta)}}{(1 + \mu - \mu G)^{\eta/(\varepsilon + \eta)}} - 1 \right].$$

Finally, in order to derive equation (IV.13) for the two-market case we note that, the quantity demanded in each market can be written as

$$D_H = k_H MR^{-\eta_H}, \qquad D_F = k_F MR^{-\eta_F}, \tag{16}$$

where

$$k_F = N_H \left(1 - \frac{1}{\eta_H} \right)^{\eta_H}, \qquad k_F = N_F \left(1 - \frac{1}{\eta_F} \right)^{\eta_F}.$$

Hence, σ in this case is expressed by

$$\sigma = \frac{D_{H_A} + D_{F_A}}{D_{H_B} + D_{F_B}} = \frac{k_H MC_A^{-\eta_H} + k_F MC_A^{-\eta_F}}{k_H MC_B^{-\eta_H} + k_F MC_B^{-\eta_F}} = \frac{MC_A^{-\eta_H} + \phi MC_A^{-\eta_H}}{MC_B^{-\eta_H} + \phi MC_B^{-\eta_H}}, \tag{17}$$

where $\phi = k_F/k_H$. But in this case

$$\phi = \frac{N_F}{N_H} \frac{[1 - (1/\eta_F)]^{\eta_F}}{[1 - (1/\eta_H)]^{\eta_H}} = \frac{Q_{F_B}}{Q_{H_B}} \frac{[MC_B^{\eta_F}]}{[MC_B^{\eta_H}]} = \theta \, MC_B^{\eta_F - \eta_H}, \tag{18}$$

where θ is a measure of market share based on sales in each market. Substituting we obtain immediately

$$\sigma = \frac{\theta}{1 + \theta} \left(\frac{MC_B}{MC_A} \right)^{\eta_H} + \frac{1}{1 + \theta} \left(\frac{MC_B}{MC_A} \right)^{\eta_F}, \tag{19}$$

which is equivalent to (IV.13).

Appendix C

Tables

TABLE 1

Property, plant, and equipment expenditures for a continuous sample, 1966–1972 and 1966 universe by three-digit industry

(thousands of dollars)

Industry (OBE)	Sample								Universe, 1966
	1966	1967	1968	1969	1970	1971	1972	1973	
Total 100	18,657	25,845	27,045	31,128	38,362	21,714	11,180	10,786	43,223
Total 200	254,050	232,109	228,417	277,929	450,944	740,456	659,979	818,747	621,124
Total 30	1,803,360	2,162,763	2,311,878	2,375,107	2,503,588	3,179,633	3,213,907	3,847,200	2,442,497
310	532,481	647,586	771,771	803,466	745,070	935,391	815,072	886,634	798,853
320	143,780	253,966	226,318	188,362	212,607	291,484	319,192	302,168	209,678
330	169,258	285,863	343,061	262,864	406,664	528,098	338,781	262,813	240,734
340	68,381	56,486	61,005	127,633	98,361	223,864	186,913	396,158	78,615
350	a	a	a	a	a	a	a	a	12,159
360	a	a	a	a	a	a	a	a	138,721
390	874,864	907,355	902,872	962,394	1,002,595	1,192,841	1,542,724	1,988,098	963,637
Total 41	121,214	138,833	129,661	153,371	139,172	130,020	148,502	189,500	289,608
411	a	a	a	a	a	a	a	a	a
412	a	a	a	a	a	a	a	a	20,032
413	16,431	16,983	15,904	22,502	23,444	19,242	29,032	38,379	33,877
414	25,247	22,426	24,098	19,506	21,755	18,600	22,080	33,539	84,356
415	a	a	a	a	a	a	a	a	a
416	a	a	a	12,658	12,353	7,859	a	15,976	53,132
418	12,499	18,995	22,066	20,807	24,856	19,760	16,647	19,025	33,806
419	34,456	38,745	a	a	a	38,196	43,520	45,592	47,843
Total 42	100,082	94,085	117,987	130,269	124,010	223,735	148,584	139,488	322,703
421	8154	21,848	7090	a	16,532	36,132	28,780	27,615	149,629
422	22,739	a	5677	a	a	a	a	a	26,171
428	a	30,413	79,326	85,475	45,940	54,066	39,164	55,721	83,076
429	a	a	25,894	22,598	a	a	a	a	63,827

	1	2	3	4	5	6	7	8	9
Total	467,815	556,748	501,253	504,602	571,824	647,714	646,911	642,556	899,485
43	40,953	37,161	33,715	34,903	46,231	58,537	72,219	68,754	79,807
431	46,007	48,035	43,692	54,591	59,291	76,447	106,483	117,657	67,186
432	a	13,964	a	a	10,069	7583	6188	10,831	19,139
433	61,919	97,270	76,890	70,640	86,780	73,401	62,290	67,357	240,617
434	118,800	125,495	98,072	117,804	150,614	240,453	197,421	169,362	214,682
435	a	49,827	a	a	33,448	15,753	10,909	14,270	74,765
436	47,761	78,147	43,953	29,420	35,702	36,848	46,804	57,146	78,082
438	105,272	106,849	130,444	160,117	149,689	138,692	144,597	137,179	125,207
439	96,374	68,571	67,724	97,181	92,200	107,425	170,889	148,844	160,961
Total	127,991	105,955	95,848	194,048	140,148	135,924	138,447	187,743	382,928
Total	10,764	a	a	a	a	21,495	11,869	20,372	40,906
44	38,672	37,188	34,126	46,661	65,017	56,312	47,993	65,893	111,445
45	a	53,981	40,548	a	52,466	a	a	a	218,675
451		a							11,902
452	663,432	666,819	585,447	777,849	1,163,942	265,809	235,954	630,314	882,627
453	42,244	93,657	87,170	70,832	77,132	81,046	67,949	145,985	46,247
459	74,607	32,100	42,895	61,299	79,323	96,455	88,011	98,779	159,663
Total	27,146	4363	a				a		95,157
46	a								
461	3150	6457	3804	6082	4898	7483	12,345	10,779	15,107
462	5686	4410	6669	8095	10,906	9514		17,111	37,326
463	5373	a	u	5097	7422	7693	5268	4943	8307
464	a								
465	118,185	121,919	112,358	156,965	222,038	215,668	226,638	308,023	238,110
466	9187	10,465	11,703	14,267	29,336	17,832	15,440	26,879	34,686
468	14,786	13,504	17,221	17,962	25,040	28,842	28,353	40,250	33,723
469	a			a	a	a	a	a	a
Total	36,188	44,706	33,265	12,225	a	71,338	82,972	101,137	52,793
47	a	9517	9674			18,658	17,605	18,101	a
471	a								27,869
472	682,514	647,839	494,169	547,948	765,947	641,314	612,400	690,362	868,595
473									
474									
478									
479									
Total									
48									

(Continued)

TABLE 1 (*Continued*)

	Industry (OBE)	Sample 1966	1967	1968	1969	1970	1971	1972	1973	Universe, 1966
Total	49	157,103	155,160	149,412	167,466	203,944	216,055	192,316	218,268	350,829
	491	13,541	9078	6387	14,306	18,778	17,707	9682	16,015	63,295
	492	15,765	8671	15,360	11,453	7678	12,190	10,929	16,762	33,720
	493	a	a	a	a	a	a	a	a	11,869
	494									4561
	495	57,182	52,046	30,708	42,662	54,786	44,478	43,444	56,763	99,305
	496	52,471	64,807	74,033	76,917	94,425	84,131	76,010	76,722	104,238
	497	a	a	a	a	a	a	a	a	10,930
	498	a	a	a	a	a	a	a		a
	499	4810	5182	5368	4622	5333	16,607	7358	10,513	a
Total	50	117,016	99,494	97,716	108,509	127,503	161,302	186,358	216,555	456,945
	521	a	a	a	a	a	a	a	a	90,819
	523	a	a	a	a	a	a	a	a	70,308
	550	a	a	a	a	a	a	a	a	137,670
	560	a	a	a	a	a	a	a	a	158,148
Total	60	156,564	178,236	206,950	241,662	343,032	328,728	428,750	454,849	399,083
	610	109,130	96,218	113,632	141,877	228,235	193,349	184,369	231,548	126,332
	631	a	042	a	569	1578	2436	a	4228	a
	632	0	a	a	a	a	a	a	a	a
	633	5491	8385	9171	16,018	16,547	25,665	40,200	33,287	19,266
	634	a	a	a	a	a	a	a	a	a
	635	751	a	387	565	816	951	1149	875	3957
	636	15,581	17,813	17,259	22,383	27,438	a	54,776	99,805	173,421
	637	3249	5267	7195	15,171	20,105	17,352	12,185	18,381	151,193
	638	4396	2046	2469	a	a	a	a	a	6822
	639	9476	a	a	a	31,823	18,837	23,071	24,106	32,881
	640	3391	5944	22,189	5296	10,458	16,081	a	14,645	10,274
Total	70–80	134,985	152,218	148,773	193,627	245,385	350,481	333,604	393,364	364,866

SOURCE: U.S. Department of Commerce, Bureau of Economic Analysis.
^a Suppressed to avoid disclosure of data for individual reporters.

TABLE 2.1

Sensitivity tests for variations in σ_i [a]

Industry number	Industry in which σ_i is raised by 1%														
	1	2	3	4	5	6	7	8	9	10	11	12	13	14	15
1	−41	−1	−7	−260	−3	−17	−2	−2	−13	−6	−12	−1	−1	−7	−10
2	0	−264	−2	−2	−1	−7	−1	−10	−17	−5	−12	0	−1	−1	−1
3	0	−2	−196	−4	−2	−17	−1	−2	−7	−3	−3	0	−1	−3	−2
4	−1	0	−2	−212	−1	−9	−1	−1	−4	−2	−3	0	0	−3	−1
5	0	−1	−7	−15	−139	−21	−4	−3	−16	−10	−11	−1	0	−7	−3
6	−1	−4	−16	−10	−8	−332	−19	−5	−23	−13	−20	−1	0	−3	−4
7	−0	−2	−4	−5	−5	−16	−91	−2	−31	−21	−28	0	−1	−2	−2
8	−1	−11	−23	−26	−7	−36	−6	−214	−320	−93	−234	−1	0	−9	−18
9	0	−14	−10	−4	−2	−9	−1	−10	−1441	−25	−108	0	−1	−3	−5
10	0	−3	−8	−3	−1	−5	−1	−5	−132	−551	−70	0	0	−4	−5
11	0	−1	−1	−1	0	−1	−1	−2	−20	−4	−768	0	−1	−1	−1
12	−1	−7	−31	−33	−25	−38	−18	−12	−90	−53	−126	−15	−2	−20	−36
13	−2	−16	−61	−39	−16	−57	−9	−20	−96	−34	−74	−1	−57	−31	−21
14	−4	−20	−71	−86	−25	−94	−17	−31	−220	−84	−152	−2	−4	−1170	−41
15	−6	−34	−193	−88	−23	−126	−18	−27	−184	−71	−139	−2	−12	−109	−438
16	0	−2	−7	−5	−2	−8	−1	−2	−15	−5	−11	0	−2	−14	−7
17	0	−1	−5	−4	−1	−5	−1	−2	−8	−3	−6	0	−4	−5	−3
18	0	0	0	0	0	0	0	0	0	0	0	0	0	0	0
19	0	0	0	0	0	0	0	0	0	0	0	0	0	0	0
20	0	0	0	0	0	0	0	0	0	0	0	0	0	0	0
21	0	0	0	0	0	0	0	0	0	0	0	0	0	0	0
Total	−57	−385	−645	−795	−260	−797	−192	−347	−2636	−984	−1779	−23	−87	−1393	−600

Change in number of jobs lost by industry

[a] Base values $\sigma_i = 1.0$; $\chi_i = 0.0$; $\gamma_{ii} = 0.0$; DFI = 1970 values.

TABLE 2.2

Sensitivity tests for variations in σ_i[a]

Industry number	Industry in which σ_i is raised by 1%														
	1	2	3	4	5	6	7	8	9	10	11	12	13	14	15
Percentage change in number of jobs lost by industry 1	−0.11	0.00	−0.02	−0.68	−0.01	−0.04	−0.01	0.00	−0.03	−0.02	−0.03	0.00	0.00	−0.02	−0.03
2	0.00	−0.81	−0.01	−0.01	0.00	−0.02	0.00	−0.03	−0.05	−0.02	−0.04	0.00	0.00	0.00	0.00
3	0.00	−0.01	−0.80	−0.02	−0.01	−0.07	−0.01	−0.01	−0.03	−0.01	−0.02	0.00	0.00	−0.01	−0.01
4	0.00	0.00	−0.01	−0.89	0.00	−0.04	0.00	0.00	−0.02	−0.01	−0.01	0.00	0.00	−0.01	0.00
5	0.00	0.00	−0.03	−0.06	−0.58	−0.09	−0.02	−0.01	−0.07	−0.04	−0.05	0.00	0.00	−0.03	−0.01
6	0.00	−0.01	−0.04	−0.02	−0.02	−0.72	−0.43	−0.01	−0.05	−0.03	−0.04	0.00	0.00	−0.01	−0.01
7	0.00	−0.01	−0.02	−0.02	−0.02	−0.08	−0.01	−0.01	−0.15	−0.10	−0.13	0.00	0.00	−0.01	−0.01
8	0.00	−0.01	−0.02	−0.03	−0.01	−0.04	0.00	−0.21	−0.32	−0.09	−0.23	0.00	0.00	0.01	−0.02
9	0.00	0.01	−0.01	0.00	0.00	−0.01	0.00	−0.01	−0.88	−0.02	−0.07	0.00	0.00	0.00	0.00
10	0.00	0.00	−0.01	0.00	0.00	−0.00	0.00	−0.01	−0.17	−0.70	−0.09	0.00	0.00	0.00	−0.01
11	0.00	0.00	0.00	0.00	0.00	−0.00	−0.03	0.00	−0.02	−0.01	−0.96	0.00	0.00	0.00	0.00
12	0.00	−0.01	−0.06	−0.07	−0.05	−0.07	−0.02	−0.02	−0.18	−0.10	−0.25	0.00	0.00	−0.04	−0.07
13	0.00	−0.03	−0.11	−0.07	−0.03	−0.11	−0.01	−0.04	−0.18	−0.06	−0.14	−0.03	−0.11	−0.06	−0.04
14	0.00	−0.01	−0.04	−0.04	−0.01	−0.05	−0.01	−0.02	−0.11	−0.04	−0.07	0.00	0.00	−0.58	−0.02
15	0.00	−0.02	−0.13	−0.06	−0.02	−0.09	0.00	−0.02	−0.13	−0.05	−0.09	0.00	−0.01	−0.07	−0.30
16	0.00	0.00	0.00	0.00	0.00	0.00	0.00	0.00	0.00	0.00	0.00	0.00	0.00	0.00	0.00
17	0.00	0.00	0.00	0.00	0.00	0.00	0.00	0.00	0.00	0.00	0.00	0.00	0.00	0.00	0.00
18	0.00	0.00	0.00	0.00	0.00	0.00	0.00	0.00	0.00	0.00	0.00	0.00	0.00	0.00	0.00
19	0.00	0.00	0.00	0.00	0.00	0.00	0.00	0.00	0.00	0.00	0.00	0.00	0.00	0.00	0.00
20	0.00	0.00	0.00	0.00	0.00	0.00	0.00	0.00	0.00	0.00	0.00	0.00	0.00	0.00	0.00
21	0.00	0.00	0.00	0.00	0.00	0.00	0.00	0.00	0.00	0.00	0.00	0.00	0.00	0.00	0.00
Total	−0.01	−0.04	−0.06	−0.07	−0.02	−0.07	−0.02	−0.03	−0.24	−0.09	−0.16	0.00	−0.01	−0.13	−0.05

[a] Base values: $\sigma_i = 1.0$; $\chi_i = 0.0$; $\gamma_i = 0.0$; DFI = 1970 values.

TABLE 3

Employment effects for 1966–1973 DFI vectors

Industry number	Total employment impact (number of jobs lost)							
	1966	1967	1968	1969	1970	1971	1972	1973
1	3821	4467	4231	4730	4751	3846	3418	3925
2	201	243	236	369	189	−157	−96	−91
3	637	704	630	676	702	709	654	662
4	6963	7726	6995	7872	6835	6117	6687	8230
5	6809	6387	7390	7855	7231	11,440	7793	7339
6	14,331	16,219	14,305	14,096	14,944	15,999	15,633	15,236
7	5639	4239	4096	5428	5062	5345	7606	6793
8	6632	6114	5983	10,256	8854	5797	5728	8700
9	28,953	28,343	24,365	31,247	48,905	8969	7736	21,203
10	10,740	10,820	9808	13,238	17,620	18,077	15,372	20,944
11	7438	6859	5117	5488	7210	5599	5199	5872
12	3367	3361	3599	4401	4439	4963	4444	5083
13	3239	3518	3392	4033	4033	3785	3377	3905
14	6328	6846	6626	7979	8374	7361	6787	8168
15	17,793	19,518	18,376	22,354	25,310	30,958	28,344	32,686
16	455	500	464	565	575	595	493	603
17	270	301	287	345	344	334	284	333
18	0	0	0	0	0	0	0	0
19	0	0	0	0	0	0	0	0
20	0	0	0	0	0	0	0	0
21	0	0	0	0	0	0	0	0
Total	123,415	126,165	115,900	140,934	160,377	126,736	119,459	149,591

[a] Here σ_i = value in column (4), Table 1, Chapter III; χ_i = historical value; $\gamma_i = 0.0$.

Appendix D

The Industry Labor Market Model

Individuals who become unemployed at a given moment in time (hereafter, called members of a "starting cohort") are assumed to draw a weekly placement probability from some probability distribution. The parameters of this distribution will in general depend on the characteristics of the particular firms and individuals that comprise the market and also on overall demand conditions.

The influence of demand conditions on placement probability values can be specified in a variety of ways. Here we assume that the jth individual's placement probability may be approximated by the following simple function of vacancy and unemployed stocks:[1]

$$p_j = k_j\left(\frac{V}{U}\right). \tag{1}$$

[1] This formulation assumes a unitary elasticity of placement probabilities with respect to the vacancy–unemployment ratio. On the basis of simple probabilistic models of the job search process this assumption appears reasonable.

Complete steady state equilibrium is defined to occur when vacancy and unemployment stocks are equal and when expected weekly accessions from the unemployed subpopulation equal weekly separations from the employed subpopulation.

We also consider the possibility of a less-than-complete equilibrium, a "quasi equilibrium" in which U exceeds V but in which separations and expected accessions are equal. In such situations, the excess of searchers over vacancies will eventually lead to falling real wages, which, in turn, will increase the quantity of labor demanded until V is brought back into balance with U.

As a practical matter, however, wages may be very slow to fall in response to an excess of searchers over vacancies. Moreover, industry labor demand may be highly wage inelastic, making possible a protracted excess of U over V. The existence of such reasonably stable disequilibrium configurations, first rationalized by Keynes in terms of wage rates being "sticky downwards," has received considerable empirical documentation in recent years and has frequently been interpreted in terms of quantity rates of adjustment strongly dominating price rates of adjustment when markets are displaced from equilibrium.[2]

Our simulation exercise considers the industry labor market to be in an initial equilibrium of the complete type. This initial equilibrium is then disturbed by industry direct foreign investment activities that simultaneously displace ΔU existing jobs and create ΔV new jobs. If E_0, U_0, and V_0 denote the employment, unemployment, and vacancy stocks prior to the disturbance, with $U_0 = V_0$, the relevant stocks immediately after the disturbance become

$$U_1 = U_0 + \Delta U, \tag{2}$$

$$V_1 = V_0 + \Delta V = U_0 + \Delta V, \tag{3}$$

and

$$E_1 = E_1 - \Delta U. \tag{4}$$

---

[2] See Leijonhuvfud (1968).

These changes in vacancy and unemployment stocks produce an immediate change in the probabilities of placement according to equation (1):

$$p_j = k_j \frac{(V_0 + \Delta V)}{(U_0 + \Delta U)}. \tag{5}$$

If the DFI-related labor demand shifts result in more workers being displaced than there are new job vacancies created, as we have estimated they do for each of the industries in our study, placement probabilities are seen from equation (5) to fall initially.

We assume that wages are slow to respond to conditions associated with the hypothesized job displacement and that policymakers do not intervene rapidly to alter the level of aggregate demand. We then trace the experience of the starting cohort period by period until the labor market establishes a quasi equilibrium of the type discussed above.

Members of the starting cohort with high placement probabilities leave unemployment rapidly while those cohort members with low placement probabilities tend to remain unemployed for longer periods of time. That is, a sorting process takes place within each starting cohort, with the result that the group of individuals who are unemployed at a given moment in time (hereafter, the "unemployed cross section") has generally lower placement probability values than do members of a starting cohort.

If starting cohort members draw their placement probability values from a beta p.d.f. with parameters x and y,[3]

$$g_0(p) = \frac{p^{x-1}(1-p)^{y-1}}{\beta(x, y)}, \tag{6}$$

it may be shown that placement probabilities of the unemployed cross section are also characterized by a beta p.d.f.,[4]

$$h_0(p) = \frac{p^{x-2}(1-p)^{y-1}}{\beta(x-1, y)}. \tag{7}$$

---

[3] Heckman and Willis (1977) have used the beta density to characterize the probabilities of labor force participation of married females. They comment in detail on the flexibility of this functional form.

[4] See Frank (1978).

Using the density assumed in (6) the mean placement probability for the starting cohort is calculated as

$$\int_0^1 pg_0(p)\,dp = \frac{x}{x+y}. \tag{8}$$

In the following discussion this mean placement probability will be denoted

$$E_{g_0}(p) = \frac{x}{x+y} = \bar{p}_{s0}. \tag{9}$$

After the hypothesized labor market disturbance, this estimate can be used to calculate the new mean placement probability for starters:

$$E_{g_1}(p) = \bar{p}_{s0}\left(\frac{U_0 + \Delta V}{U_0 + \Delta U}\right) = \bar{p}_{s0}\left(\frac{V_1}{U_1}\right). \tag{10}$$

The predisturbance mean placement probability for the unemployed cross section is computed from equation (7) as

$$E_{h_0}(p) = \frac{x-1}{x+y-1} = \bar{p}_{u0}. \tag{11}$$

Equation (11) implies a postdisturbance mean placement probability for the unemployed cross section of

$$E_{h_1}(p) = \bar{p}_{u0}\left(\frac{V_1}{U_1}\right). \tag{12}$$

After the first week of search, the expected number of accessions to employment from a starting cohort of size ΔU can be calculated using the mean placement probability value given in equation (10)

$$a_{s1} = \Delta U \cdot \bar{p}_{s0}\left(\frac{V_1}{U_1}\right). \tag{13}$$

At the end of the same week, the expected number of accessions from the unemployed cross section (exclusive of the ΔU starters) is

$$a_{u1} = U_0 \bar{p}_{u0}\left(\frac{V_1}{U_1}\right). \tag{14}$$

Total separations after the first week of search, denoted s_1, are assumed to be generated by an exogenously determined separations rate, t:

$$s_1 = tE_1. \tag{15}$$

The next step in the simulation exercise is to generate second-week stock values by combining the first-week stock values given in equations (2)–(4) with the first-week transition values given in equations (13)–(15):

$$U_2 = U_1 - a_{s1} - a_{u1} + s_1, \tag{16}$$

$$V_2 = V_1 - a_{s1} - a_{u1} + s_1, \tag{17}$$

and

$$E_2 = E_1 - s_1 + a_{s1} + a_{u1}. \tag{18}$$

It is also convenient at this point to decompose the unemployed stock into two substocks, (1) the remainder of the original ΔU workers displaced by DFI and (2) all other unemployed persons:

$$U_{s2} = \Delta U - a_{s1}, \tag{19}$$

and

$$U_{u2} = U_2 - a_{s2}. \tag{20}$$

These stocks are in turn used as inputs into the calculation of second-period transitions.

Second-week accessions from the unemployed cross section are routinely computed by using second-week unemployed and vacancy stocks in equation (1) and substituting as in equation (14):

$$a_{u2} = U_{2u} \bar{P}_{u0} \left(\frac{V_2}{U_2} \right). \tag{21}$$

The procedure for calculating second-week transitions from the remainder of the starting cohort requires an adjustment in the p.d.f. for the original cohort. This adjustment is necessary to account for the fact that the first-week job finders who have been eliminated from the starting cohort do not constitute a random sample from that group. Instead, they are a weighted sample, where the weights are proportional to individual placement probability values. The second-week survivors are the residual when this weighted sample is eliminated from the original group. Abstracting from effects having to do with total vacancy and unemployed stocks, the second-week survivors placement probability p.d.f. is related to the original p.d.f. by

$$g_2(p) = \frac{(1 - p)}{1 - E_{g_1}(p)} g_1(p), \tag{22}$$

where $E_{g_1}(p)$ denotes the mean p value inplied by $g_1(p)$.[5]

Using equation (22), the mean placement probability for second-week survivors, adjusted for second-week values of vacancy and employed stocks, is

$$E_{g_2}(p) = \left(\frac{V_2}{U_2}\right) \int_0^1 p g_2(p) \, dp. \tag{23}$$

This mean placement probability value is then used to calculate the expected number of accessions from the second-week survivors of the starting cohort:

$$a_{s2} = U_{s2} E_{g_2}(p). \tag{24}$$

Second-week separations are computed as

$$s_2 = t E_2. \tag{25}$$

Third and subsequent week stocks and flows are calculated using procedures exactly parallel to those used for the second-week magnitudes.

The short-run outcome of these iterative calculations is the establishment of a quasi equilibrium in which the flow of accessions equals the flow of separations but in which the stock of job searchers persists at a

---

[5] See Frank (1978). The mean placement probability implied by $g_1(p)$ generally will be higher than the corresponding mean p value for the unemployed cross section. The placement probability p.d.f. for nth week survivors in the starting cohort is derived in a completely analogous fashion from the p.d.f. for the previous week's survivors. As individuals with high placement probabilities continue to leave a particular starting cohort, the mean placement probability value of surviving members of that cohort will eventually fall below that of the unemployed cross section, whose membership is continuously replenished by new starting cohorts.

higher level than the stock of vacancies. This quasi-equilibrium position is defined formally by

$$tE^* = E_h(p^*)U^*,\tag{26}$$

where the starred variables represent values taken in the quasi-equilibrium position and where

$$E_h(p^*) = \bar{p}_{u0}\,\frac{V^*}{U^*},\tag{27}$$

is the quasi-equilibrium mean placement probability for the unemployed cross section.

Substituting equations (11) and (27) into (26) yields

$$tE^* = \bar{p}_{u0}\,V^*.\tag{28}$$

The quantities V^* and E^* are also related by

$$E^* + V^* = J^*,\tag{29}$$

where

$$J^* = E_0 + V_0 - \Delta U + \Delta V,\tag{30}$$

total demand for labor in the quasi-equilibrium position.

Solving (28) and (29), we obtain

$$E^* = \left(\frac{\bar{p}_{u0}}{t + \bar{p}_{u0}}\right)J^*,\tag{31}$$

and

$$V^* = \left(\frac{t}{t + \bar{p}_{u0}}\right)J^*.\tag{32}$$

Since the labor force is assumed to have remained unchanged, we also have

$$U^* + E^* = U_0 + E_0,\tag{33}$$

so that

$$U^* = U_0 + (E_0 - E^*).\tag{34}$$

The mean placement probability for the starting cohort in the quasi-equilibrium position is given by

$$E_g(p^*) = \bar{p}_{s0}\left(\frac{V^*}{U^*}\right). \tag{35}$$

The average duration of completed spells for members of a pre-disturbance starting cohort is given by[6]

$$\bar{d}_{s0} = \sum_{T=1}^{\infty} T\left(\int_0^1 p_0(1 - p_0)^{T-1}g(p_0)dp_0\right). \tag{36}$$

The corresponding average duration for the quasi-equilibrium position is

$$\bar{d}_s^* = \sum_{T-1}^{\infty} T\left(\int_0^1 p^*(1 - p^*)^{T-1}g(p^*)\,dp\right), \tag{37}$$

where $p^* = (V^*/U^*)p$.

As long as the duration of unemployment remains higher than its initial value following a DFI-related disturbance, all workers who enter the pool of job seekers, whether because of a DFI displacement or not, can expect to experience a lengthier spell of unemployment than they would have in the absence of the disturbance. Put another way, there will continue to be more people unemployed on the average than there were originally, even well after most of the initially displaced workers have secured new jobs. In terms of the quasi-equilibrium position described above, there will be U^* people unemployed each period as compared with the initial equilibrium value U_0. The difference,

$$U^* - U_0 = (\Delta U - \Delta V)\left(\frac{\bar{p}_{u0}}{t + \bar{p}_{u0}}\right), \tag{38}$$

we will label the residual contribution to industry unemployment of the DFI-related disturbance. This residual contribution will persist as long as the quasi-equilibrium condition persists; that is, until falling wages, a sectoral product demand shift, aggregate policies, or some other phenomenon occurs so as to reestablish the industry balance between vacancies and unemployment.

[6] See Frank (1978).

Data Sources for the Simulation Exercise

The year 1970 was chosen for our simulation exercise because the overall unemployment rate of 4.9 % during that year approximates the "full employment" level characteristic of contemporary macroeconomic policy discussions.

Employment and Earnings publishes data for employment (E_0) and unemployment (U_0) for most important manufacturing industries at the level of aggregation corresponding to our employment demand estimates reported in Chapter V.

The parameters of the placement probability p.d.f.'s for the starting cohort and the unemployed cross section are adapted from Frank (1978), where it was estimated that for a 1974 starting cohort of household heads

$$g_0(p) = \beta(x, y) = \beta(5.2, 40.1). \tag{39}$$

Though aggregate demand was somewhat more sluggish in 1974 than in 1970, the average duration of unemployment reported by the Bureau of Labor Statistics was exactly the same for 1974 household heads as for 1970 manufacturing workers (9.7 weeks).[7]

For computational convenience, this continuous probability density was approximated by the discrete p.d.f. shown in Fig. 1.

A discrete approximation to the corresponding p.d.f. for the unemployed cross section,

$$h_0(p) = \beta(x - 1, y) = \beta(4.2, 40.1) \tag{40}$$

was also constructed and is shown in Fig. 2 below.

The discrete densities displayed in Figs. 1 and 2 were then adjusted in the following manner in an attempt to reflect interindustry differences in placement probabilities that existed in 1970. First, the 1970 average

---

[7] The unemployment duration concept used by the BLS is the mean duration to date of all unemployment spells currently in process. Because persons with unusually long unemployment spells are greatly overrepresented in the sample of currently unemployed persons, this magnitude substantially overstates the average duration of all completed spells of unemployment that occur.

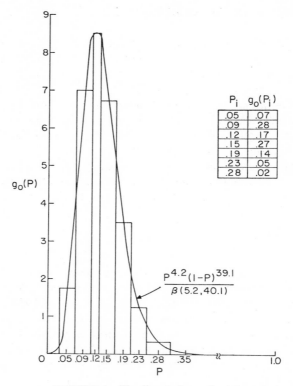

P_i	$g_0(P_i)$
.05	.07
.09	.28
.12	.17
.15	.27
.19	.14
.23	.05
.28	.02

FIGURE 1   The discrete form of $g_0(p)$.

duration of unemployment (measured in months) for each manufacturing industry was calculated using the relationship[8]

$$d_j = \frac{U_j}{\tau_j}, \tag{41}$$

where U_j is the 1970 unemployment rate for the jth industry and τ_j is the jth industry separations rate (separations per month per 100

[8] Separations rate figures were not available for the paper, chemical, and rubber industries. For these industries, equation (41) was computed using the unemployment and separations rates for all nondurable manufacturing industries.

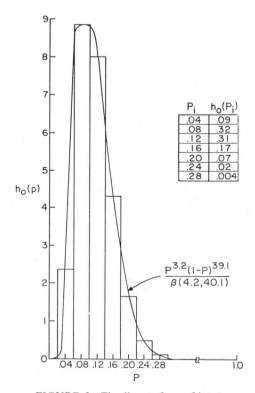

P_i	$h_0(P_i)$
.04	.09
.08	.32
.12	.31
.16	.17
.20	.07
.24	.02
.28	.004

$$\frac{P^{3.2}(1-P)^{39.1}}{\beta(4.2, 40.1)}$$

FIGURE 2   The discrete form of $h_0(p)$.

employees).[9] For the jth industry, placement probabilities in the densities shown in Figs. 1 and 2 were then transformed according to

$$p_{ij} = p_{i0}\left(\frac{\bar{d}}{d_j}\right), \qquad (42)$$

where $\bar{d}$ is the average duration of 1970 unemployment spells in manufacturing computed as shown in equation (41).

---

[9] The expression τ_j in equation (41) is slightly different from the expression t in equation (43). The former includes direct transitions from one job to another while the latter does not. We assume that the patterns of interindustry variations are the same for the two turnover concepts.

The separations rate for the jth industry was calculated as

$$t_j = \frac{\bar{p}_{u0} U_0}{E_0}. \tag{43}$$

Our first calculations in the simulation exercise trace the placement probability movements in weekly intervals and employ these values to compute time profiles of the number of DFI-displaced workers who remain unemployed in each industry. These are the "direct unemployment effects" summarized in Tables 1 and 2 in Chapter VII. The properties of the quasi equilibrium are summarized as "indirect unemployment effects" in Table 3 in Chapter VII.

When interpreting the results reported in Tables 1–3 in Chapter VII, several qualifications should be borne in mind.

As the exercise was set up, all of the dislocations resulting from both the direct and indirect effects of the 1970 DFI vector were presumed to have occurred all at once. One might easily argue that, at the level of industry aggregation of our study, DFI effects would be better characterized as occurring in a smooth flow throughout the year. The effect of such a characterization is to replace the large groups of unemployed workers whose experience we trace in Tables 1 and 2 in Chapter VII with many smaller groups. The unemployment profiles of these smaller groups will be very much like those of the larger groups and, as the DFI accumulates to its yearly total, the residual unemployment contribution under the smooth flow view becomes identical with its lump-sum approach counterpart.

Actual implementation of our model required first that certain assumptions be made concerning the nature of the export displacement and export stimulus effects discussed in Chapter III. If the foreign investment project is preceded by a complete shutdown of the domestic production facility, whereupon a domestic operation is reorganized to serve the export requirements of the foreign production site, the number of initially displaced workers is determined by size of the export displacement effect, while the number of new vacancies will be determined by the size of the export stimulus effect. On the other hand, if the U.S. export requirements of the overseas production site are satisfied by simply retaining some portion of the domestic production operation intact, the number of initially displaced workers is determined by the difference between the export stimulus and export displacement effects, while the number of new vacancies would be zero. The actual mix of these two assumptions that best characterizes the industries in our study would be quite difficult to estimate precisely. For the purposes of our calculations in Chapter VII we have assumed the maximally dislocative alternative, namely that U.S. export requirements of foreign production sites are served from newly organized domestic operations. In interpreting our findings, therefore, it should be kept in mind that our estimates of the number of initially displaced workers are, at least on this particular account, upward biased. Since the export stimulus is usually only a small fraction of the export displacement, however, this bias is probably very small.

A very similar qualification applies in the case when the overseas production transfer occurs in the context of a firm whose domestic employment is growing rapidly. For such firms, the export displacement effect may take the form of fewer new workers being hired rather than existing employees being discharged. If so, our estimates of the initially displaced workers will again be upward biased.

As far as the residual unemployment estimates are concerned, however, these depend only on the size of the net employment demand reduction (i.e., the difference between the export displacement and export stimulus effects) and will thus be affected neither by the particular assumptions made about whether the export stimulus effect requires the reorganization of domestic production facilities nor by the rate of growth of domestic employment demand.

The concept of placement probabilities used in the simulation may constitute an additional source of upward bias in our estimates of the short-run dislocations caused by DFI. The placement probability p.d.f.'s shown in equations (39) and (40) were estimated under a framework that overlooks transitions from one job to another that do not involve an intervening spell of unemployment. Our procedures thus assume implicitly that no worker whose job is displaced by DFI will relocate immediately in another job. To the extent that some displaced workers are able to line up new jobs before leaving their old ones, however, the values in Tables 1 and 2 of Chapter VII should be adjusted downward.

Finally, in our model it was assumed that industry labor markets were essentially independent of one another. In practice, however, we may witness substantial interindustry migration on the part of job seekers, the effect of which would be to eliminate much of what limited heterogeneity is displayed in the collection of adjustment paths in Tables 1 and 2 of Chapter VII.

Appendix E

Sensitivity Tests

In Tables 1 and 2 we show the results of selected partial sensitivity tests on the two versions of the DFI model used in the text. With the exception of the tests in rows 2 and 3, the experiment performed is parallel to that of the "base value" experiment. In each case we have solved the system (by numerical search) to find the technology gap values that produce a steady state equilibrium in which the overseas stock of U.S. owned capital equals 6% of the total U.S. owned stock. We then compare, as before, the levels of variables in that steady state with those in the autarky steady state. Definitions of entries are identical to those given in Table 1 of Chapter VIII. The sensitivity tests differ from the base value case only in that in each sensitivity test one parameter is varied from its baselevel value.

Inasmuch as the tests are in all other respects the same, the entries in Tables 1 and 2 provide a measure of the stability of our results. For

147

TABLE 1 *Sensitivity tests—Aggregate savings model*

	Change in U.S. national income (%)	Change in U.S. rate of return (%)	Change in U.S. wages (%)	Change in labor's share of national income (%)
1. Base values	0.53	−5.86	3.35	1.24
2. $[(k - e)/e] = 0.066$ (+10%)	0.58	−6.41	3.67	1.36
3. $\lambda = 0.942$ (+0.7%)	0.39	−4.16	2.33	0.86
4. $\rho = 0.825$ (+10%)	0.54	−5.37	3.04	1.24
5. $\omega = 0.479$ (+3.9%)	0.58	−5.76	3.50	1.25
6. $\tau = 0.473$ (+10%)	0.68	−5.98	3.42	1.18
7. $\tau^* = 0.440$ (+10%)	0.68	−6.01	3.43	1.19
8. $t = 0.473$ (+10%)	0.38	−5.72	3.26	1.30
9. $t, \tau = 0.473$ (both +10%)	0.53	−5.87	3.35	1.24
10. "risk premium" = 0.225 (−10%)	0.60	−5.92	3.38	1.21
11. $\zeta = 0.176$ (+10%)	0.53	−5.88	3.36	1.25
12. $\eta = 0.077$ (+10%)	0.54	−5.85	3.34	1.23
13. $k^* = 3.47$ (+1.7%)	0.54	−5.90	3.37	1.25
14. $\theta = 0.44$ (+10%)	0.53	−5.80	3.31	1.22
15. $\lambda\mu = 0.9$ (−10%)	0.54	−5.91	3.37	1.25

TABLE 2 *Sensitivity tests—Disaggregated savings model*

	Change in U.S. national income (%)	Change in U.S. rate of return (%)	Change in U.S. wages (%)	Change in labor's share of national income (%)
1. Base values	−3.00	2.88	−1.51	1.23
2. $[(k - e)/e] = 0.66$ (+10%)	−3.31	3.16	−1.65	1.36
3. $\lambda = 0.960$ (+0.46%)		no convergence		
4. $\rho = 0.825$ (+10%)	−3.08	2.78	−1.46	1.23
5. $\omega = 0.479$ (+3.9%)	−3.33	3.34	−1.85	1.25
6. $\tau = 0.473$ (+10%)	−2.82	2.54	−1.34	1.20
7. $\tau^* = 0.440$ (+10%)	−3.08	3.26	−1.70	1.19
8. $t = 0.473$ (+10%)	−2.93	2.43	−1.28	1.30
9. $t, \tau = 0.473$ (both +10%)	−2.73	2.12	−1.12	1.24
10. "risk premium" = 0.225 (−10%)	−2.85	2.61	−1.37	1.20
11. $\zeta_F = 0.01$	−3.02	2.90	−1.52	1.24
12. $\eta = 0.077$ (+10%)	−2.61	1.89	−1.00	1.22
13. $k^* = 3.47$ (+1.71%)	−3.00	2.88	−1.51	1.23
14. $\theta = 0.44$	−3.02	2.89	−1.52	1.24
15. $\delta = 0.052$ (+4%)	−3.31	3.16	−1.65	1.36

convenience, we have shifted the parameter values by an arbitrary 10 % (when appropriate and feasible) in order to get a significant degree of variation. Although this procedure facilitates intertest comparisons, one should not infer that 10 % changes (or errors) in all parameters are equally likely. Our estimate of the domestic corporate tax rate τ, for example, is certainly more reliable than that of, say, the foreign capital/labor ratio k^*.

As can be seen in Table 1, the findings from the aggregated savings version of the model appear to be quite stable to shifts in the model's basic parameters. The greatest variations are associated with parameters that affect the two regimes in a differential fashion, such as tax rates, the "risk premium" on foreign investment, and to a lesser extent, ω. Changes in the growth rate of labor, the savings rate, and the foreign sector parameters have a rather mild impact on the comparison between steady states. It is also worth pointing out that when both the tax on domestic returns and the tax on foreign returns are increased simultaneously in row 9 (corresponding under the present tax system to a higher U.S. tax on corporate profits without regard to source), the effects are also considerably less pronounced. In short, in this version of the model it appears that parameters affecting the intraperiod allocation of factors have a more significant impact than those that bear primarily on dynamic adjustment.

Although the tests in Table 2 also show relatively little variation on the whole, the pattern of effects is rather different. Tax rate changes have only a moderate impact on the results, with the strongest effect seen in the case in which both τ and t are raised (row 9, again). Changes in the growth rate of labor, the depreciation allowance, and ω have a comparatively strong effect. As before, shifts in foreign-sector variables are a less important source of variation. This pattern suggests that this version of the model is especially sensitive to changes in variables that affect the dynamic adjustment, either directly or through the distributional effects of DFI on income components.

Several of the tests merit separate comment. Row 8 in both tables shows the partial effect of a shift in t, the total tax on DFI earnings. Although these results apply to a 10 % *increase* in t, they may be used to infer the order of magnitude of error introduced by ignoring U.S. tax deferral on overseas-earned income. With the present parameters an indefinite (i.e., permanent) deferral would be equivalent to a value of t equal to 0.40, the base level of τ^*. This amounts to about an 8 % decline in t. Accordingly, the figures in row 9 of Tables 1 and 2 suggest that the magnitude of the error introduced by ignoring deferral is not large. The direction of error, however, depends on whether one favors the first or second model.

In Chapter VIII we discussed the fact that our method of solution requires solving the system for the unknown technology-gap parameters, using estimates of the other parameters and an observation on the ratio of foreign-invested capital to total capital stock. This requires postulating a relationship between these two parameters (λ and μ) that in a rough sense distributes the total gap over the two types of technology differences. For lack of any better hypothesis, in the "base value" runs this relationship was assumed to be $\lambda\mu = 1.0$, i.e., technology gaps of equal size. In row 15 we have tested the sensitivity of our results to this assumption by redoing the exercise for $\lambda\mu = 0.9$, and find that the change has relatively little effect.

Finally, in row 11 of Table 2 we relax our assumption of equilibrium in the basic balance, in favor of 1 % (of GNP) deficit in both regimes. Again, the results do not appear to be particularly sensitive to changes in this assumption.

Before concluding, it is important to point out that these tests investigate only the effects on our *comparison* of steady states. As such, they provide some information about the degree of error in this comparison introduced by inaccuracies in the model's parameters. On balance, the error does not appear to be very large.

They do not reveal, however, whether or not the steady states themselves are sensitive to changes in the model. Various experiments with the model (not reported here) have shown that, in fact, the steady states are rather sensitive to the choice of savings rates, growth rates, and production parameters; they are less so to changes in tax levels and foreign-sector variables. Some indirect evidence of this point is seen in rows 2 and 3 of Tables 1 and 2. In row 2 of both tables we have assumed that the ratio of steady state, foreign-invested capital stock is one-tenth higher (6.6 % instead of 6.0 %). In row 3, we vary the technology parameters without constraining the steady state capital stock ratio to 6.0 %. Hence, except for differences in scale the two experiments are in a sense mirror images of one another. The latter experiment in particular produces rather large swings in the steady state values—especially for the disaggregated model which failed to converge on a solution for a relatively small change in λ. (The test varied $(1 - \lambda)$ by 10%.) This suggests, of course, that in using these models, even if only for comparison of steady states, care must be taken not only to specify parameters accurately, but also to insure that the model is not forced into an implausible range.

References

Adler, M., and Stevens, G. V. G. (1974). "The Trade Effects of Direct Investment," *Journal of Finance*, May.

Alterman, J. (1965). "Interindustry Employment Requirements," *Monthly Labor Review*, July.

Baldwin, R. E. (1970). *Non-tariff Distortions of International Trade*, The Brookings Institution, Washington, D.C.

Baranson, J. (1970). "Technology Transfer, and the Multinational Firm," *American Economic Review Papers and Proceedings*, May.

Baranson, J. (1978). "Technology Transfer: Effects on U.S. Competitiveness and Employment," in *The Impact of International Trade and Investment on Employment* (W. Dewald, ed.). U.S. Government Printing Office, Washington, D.C., forthcoming.

Belli, D. R., Allnutt, S. W., and Murad, H. (1973). "Property, Plant and Equipment Expenditures by Majority-Owned Foreign Affiliates of U.S. Companies: Revised Estimates for 1966–72 and Projections for 1973 and 1974," *Survey of Current Business*, December.

Brems, H. (1970). "A Growth Model of International Direct Investment," *American Economic Review*, June.

Bureau of Economic Analysis, Department of Commerce (1974). "The Input–Output Structure of the U.S. Economy: 1964," *Survey of Current Business*, February.

Business International, Inc. (1972). *The Effects of U.S. Corporate Direct Foreign Investment 1960–1970*. New York.

Cantor, A. (1972). "Tax Subsidies that Export Jobs," *AFL-CIO American Federationist*, November.

153

Caves, R. (1971). "International Corporations: The Industrial Economics of Foreign Investment," *Economica*, February.

Chipman, J. (1972). "The Theory of Exploitative Trade and Investment Policy: A Reformation and Synthesis," in *International Economics and Development* (L. E. DiMarco, ed.). Academic Press, New York.

Christensen, L., and Jorgenson, D. (1969). "The Measurement of the U.S. Real Capital Input, 1929–1967," *Review of Income and Wealth*, December.

Contracting Parties to the General Agreement on Tariffs and Trade (1970). *Basic Documentation for Tariff Study*, Summary Table No. 2, Tariff and Trade Profiles by Product Categories, Geneva.

Cook, P., and Frank, R. (1975). "The Effect of Unemployment Dispersion on the Rate of Wage Inflation," *Journal of Monetary Economics*, April.

Emergency Committee for American Trade (1973). *The Multinational Corporation: American Mainstay in the World Economy*, New York.

Frank, R. (1978). "How Long Is a Spell of Unemployment," *Econometrica*, March.

Frank, R., and Freeman, R. (1978). "The Distributional Consequences of Direct Foreign Investment," in *The Impact of International Trade and Investment on Employment* (W. Dewald, ed.), U.S. Government Printing Office, Washington, D.C., forthcoming.

Freeman, R. (1974). *Technology Differences and Patterns of Foreign Trade and Investment*, unpublished Ph.D. dissertation, Stanford University.

Frenkel, J. (1971). "A Dynamic Analysis of the Balance of Payments in A Model of Accumulation," *Journal of International Economics*, May.

Frenkel, J., and Fischer, S. (1972). "International Capital Movements Along Balanced Growth Paths," *Economic Record*, June.

Gruber, W., Mehta, D., and Vernon, R. (1967). "The R & D Factor in International Trade and International Investment of United States Industries, *Journal of Political Economy*, February.

Hall, R. (1972). "Turnover in the Labor Force," *Brookings Papers on Economic Activity*, 3.

Harberger (1978). "Comment," in *The Impact of International Trade and Investment on Employment* (W. Dewald, ed.). U.S. Government Printing Office, Washington, D.C., forthcoming.

Hawkins, R. G. (1972a). "U.S. Multinational Investment in Manufacturing and Domestic Economic Performance," Occasional Paper No. 1, Center for Multinational Studies, Washington, D.C., February.

Hawkins, R. G. (1972b). "Job Displacement and the Multinational Firm: A Methodological Review," Occasional Paper No. 3, New York: Center for Multinational Studies, New York University, June.

Heckman, J. and Willis, R. J. (1977). "A Beta Logistic Model for the Analysis of Sequential Labor Force Participation, *Journal of Political Economy*, February.

Herring, R., and Willett, T. D. (1973). "The Relationship Between U.S. Direct Investment at Home and Abroad," *Revista Internazionale Sci. Econ. Com.*, January.

Horst, T. (1971). "The Theory of the Multinational Firm: Optimal Behavior Under Different Tariff and Tax Rates," *Journal of Political Economy*, September–October.

Horst, T. (1972a). "The Industrial Composition of U.S. Exports and Subsidiary Sales to the Canadian Market," *American Economic Review*, March.

Horst, T. (1972b). "Firm and Industry Determinants of the Decision to Invest Abroad: An Empirical Study," *Review of Economics and Statistics*, August.

Horst, T. (1973). "The Simple Analytics of Multinational Firm Behavior," in *International Trade and Money* (M. Connolly and A. Swoboda, eds.). University of Toronto Press, Toronto.

Horst, T. (1974). "American Exports and Foreign Direct Investments." Harvard Institute of Economic Research, Discussion Paper No. 362, May.

Hufbauer, G. (1975). "The Multinational Corporation and Direct Investment," in *International Trade and Finance* (P. Kenen, ed.). Cambridge University Press, London and New York.

Hufbauer, G., and Adler, M. (1968). *Overseas Manufacturing Investment and the Balance of Payments*. U.S. Treasury Department, Washington, D.C.

Hymer, S. (1976). *The International Operations of National Firms: A Study of Direct Foreign Investment*, MIT Press, Cambridge, Massachusetts.

Hymer, S., and Rowthorne, R. (1970). "Multinational Corporations and International Oligopoly: The Non-American Challenge," in *The International Corporation* (C. Kindleberger, ed.), MIT Press Cambridge, Massachusetts.

Jones, R. (1967). "International Capital Movements and the Theory of Tariffs and Trade," *Quarterly Journal of Economics*, February.

Kemp, J. (1966). "The Gains from International Trade and Investment: A Neo-Heckscher-Ohlin Approach," *American Economic Review*, September.

Kemp, M. (1969). *The Pure Theory of International Trade*. Prentice Hall, Englewood Cliffs, New Jersey.

Kindleberger, C. (1969). *American Business Abroad*. Yale Univ. Press, New Haven, Connecticut.

Kindleberger, C. (ed.) (1970). *The International Corporation*. MIT Press, Cambridge, Massachusetts.

Koizumi, T., and Kopecky, K. (1977). "Economic Growth, Capital Movements, and the International Transfer of Technical Knowledge," *Journal of International Economics*, February.

Kraseman, T. W., and Barker, B. L. (1973). "Employment and Payroll Costs of U.S. Multinational Companies," *Survey of Current Business*, October.

Krause, L., and Dam, K. (1964). *Federal Tax Treatment of Foreign Income*. The Brookings Institution, Washington, D.C.

Leijonhuvfud, A. (1968). *On Keynesian Economics and the Economics of Keynes*. Oxford Univ. Press, London and New York.

Lipsey, R. G. (1960). "The Relation Between Unemployment and the Rate of Change of Money Wages in the United Kingdom, 1862–1957—Further Analysis," *Economica*, February.

Lipsey, R. E., and Weiss, M. Y. (1969). "The Relation of U.S. Manufacturing Abroad to U.S. Exports: A Framework for Analysis," 1969 Business and Economic Statistics Section, *Proceedings of the American Statistical Association*.

Magee, S. (1977). "Information and the Multinational Corporation: An Appropriability Theory of Direct Foreign Investment," in *The New International Economic Order—The North-South Debate*, MIT Press, Cambridge, Massachusetts.

Morley, S., and Smith, J. (1977a). "The Choice of Technology: Multinational Firms in Brazil," *Economic Development and Cultural Change*, January.

Morley, S., and Smith, J. (1977b). "Limited Search and Technology Choices of Multinational Firms in Brazil," *Quarterly Journal of Economics*, May.

Musgrave, P. (1966). *United States Taxation of Foreign Investment Income: Issues and Arguments*. Harvard University Law School, Cambridge, Massachusetts.

Musgrave, P. (1975). *Direct Investment Abroad and the Multinationals: Effects on the United States Economy*, study prepared for the U.S. Senate Committee on Foreign Relations (Subcommittee on Multinational Corporations), U.S. Government Printing Office, Washington, D.C., August.

National Foreign Trade Council (1971). *The Impact of U.S. Direct Foreign Investment on U.S. Employment and Trade*. National Foreign Trade Council, Inc., New York, November.

Neher, P. (1970). "International Capital Movements Along Balanced Growth Paths," *Economic Record*, September.

Perry, G. (1972). "Unemployment Flows in the U.S. Labor Market," *Brookings Papers on Economic Activity*, **2**.

Polk, J., Meister, I., and Veit, L. (1966). *U.S. Production Abroad and the Balance of Payments*, The Conference Board, New York.

Ray, E. (1977). "Foreign Direct Investment in Manufacturing," *Journal of Political Economy*, April.

Rodriguez, C. (1975). "Trade in Technological Knowledge and the National Advantage," *Journal of Political Economy*, January–February.

Salant, S. (1977). "Search Theory and Duration Data: A Theory of Sorts," *Quarterly Journal of Economics*, February.

Scaperlanda, A. E., and Mauer, L. J. (1969). "The Determinants of U.S. Direct Investment in the EEC, *American Economic Review*, September.

Statistical Office of the United Nations (1970). *Statistical Yearbook*, New York.

Stevens, G. V. G. (1969). "Fixed Investment Expenditures of Foreign Manufacturing Affiliates of U.S. Firms: Theoretical Models and Empirical Evidence," *Yale Economic Essays*, Spring.

Stobaugh, R. B. (1972). "How Investment Abroad Creates Jobs at Home," *Harvard Business Review*, **50**, September–October.

Stobaugh, R. B., and Associates (1972). *U.S. Multinational Enterprises and the U.S. Economy: A Research Study of the Major Industries That Account for 90 Percent of U.S. Foreign Direct Investment in Manufacturing*, Harvard Graduate School of Business Administration, Boston, Massachusetts.

Suits, D. (1970). *Principles of Economics*. Harper, New York.

Teece, D. (1977). "Technology Transfer by Multinational Firms," *Economic Journal*, June.

U.S. Department of Commerce (1970). *Special Survey of U.S. Multinational Companies for 1970*.

U.S. Tariff Commission (1973). *Implications of Multinational Firms for World Trade and Investment and for U.S. Trade and Labor.* Report to the U.S. Senate Committee on Finance, February.

Vernon, R. (1966). "International Investment and International Trade in the Product Cycle," *Quartely Journal of Economics,* May.

Wan, H. (1971). *Economic Growth.* Harcourt Brace Jovanovich, Inc., New York.

ECONOMIC THEORY, ECONOMETRICS, AND MATHEMATICAL ECONOMICS

Consulting Editor: Karl Shell

UNIVERSITY OF PENNSYLVANIA
PHILADELPHIA, PENNSYLVANIA

Franklin M. Fisher and Karl Shell. **The Economic Theory of Price Indices:** *Two Essays on the Effects of Taste, Quality, and Technological Change*

Luis Eugenio Di Marco (Ed.). International Economics and Development: *Essays in Honor of Raúl Presbisch*

Erwin Klein. Mathematical Methods in Theoretical Economics: *Topological and Vector Space Foundations of Equilibrium Analysis*

Paul Zarembka (Ed.). Frontiers in Econometrics

George Horwich and Paul A. Samuelson (Eds.). Trade, Stability, and Macro-economics: *Essays in Honor of Lloyd A. Metzler*

W. T. Ziemba and R. G. Vickson (Eds.). Stochastic Optimization Models in Finance

Steven A. Y. Lin (Ed.). Theory and Measurement of Economic Externalities

David Cass and Karl Shell (Eds.). The Hamiltonian Approach to Dynamic Economics

R. Shone. Microeconomics: *A Modern Treatment*

C. W. J. Granger and Paul Newbold. Forecasting Economic Time Series

Michael Szenberg, John W. Lombardi, and Eric Y. Lee. Welfare Effects of Trade Restrictions: *A Case Study of the U.S. Footwear Industry*

Haim Levy and Marshall Sarnat (Eds.). Financial Decision Making under Uncertainty

Yasuo Murata. Mathematics for Stability and Optimization of Economic Systems

Alan S. Blinder and Philip Friedman (Eds.). Natural Resources, Uncertainty, and General Equilibrium Systems: *Essays in Memory of Rafael Lusky*

Jerry S. Kelly. Arrow Impossibility Theorems

Peter Diamond and Michael Rothschild (Eds.). Uncertainty in Economics: *Readings and Exercises*

Fritz Machlup. Methodology of Economics and Other Social Sciences

Robert H. Frank and Richard T. Freeman. **Distributional Consequences of Direct Foreign Investment**

In preparation

Elhanan Helpman and Assaf Razin. **A Theory of International Trade Under Uncertainty**

Marc Nerlove, David M. Grether, and José L. Carvalho. **Analysis of Economic Time Series:** *A Synthesis*

Thomas J. Sargent. **Macroeconomic Theory**